I0568795

Sustainable Energy

A Practical Guide to Sustainable Community Development

(How to Save Money Using Renewable Energy, Living Green and Living Sustainably)

Marquis Foster

Published By **Chris David**

Marquis Foster

All Rights Reserved

Sustainable Energy: A Practical Guide to Sustainable Community Development (How to Save Money Using Renewable Energy, Living Green and Living Sustainably)

ISBN   978-1-998901-30-2

No part of this guidebook shall be reproduced in any form without permission in writing from the publisher except in the case of brief quotations embodied in critical articles or reviews.

Legal & Disclaimer

The information contained in this ebook is not designed to replace or take the place of any form of medicine or professional medical advice. The information in this ebook has been provided for educational & entertainment purposes only.

The information contained in this book has been compiled from sources deemed reliable, and it is accurate to the best of the Author's knowledge; however, the Author cannot guarantee its accuracy and validity and cannot be held liable for any errors or omissions. Changes are periodically made to this book. You must consult your doctor or get professional medical advice before using any of the suggested remedies, techniques, or information in this book.

Table of contents

Chapter 1: What Is Solar Energy?

Solar electricity is the electricity associated with sun radiation and is the most substantial electricity deliver on Earth. In fact, the whole amount of sun electricity incident on our planet a protracted manner exceeds the arena's modern-day and projected destiny energy dreams.

It may be applied in quite a few techniques, in particular to generate electricity or thermal electricity for homes, public homes, and additional.

In the coming years, sun strength is predicted to emerge as an more and more used power deliver due to its characteristic of being absolutely inexhaustible and, really, an entire lot much less polluting, in sharp evaluation to confined and immoderate environmental effect fossil fuels which incorporates coal, oil and natural gasoline.

But wherein does all this energy come from? Our Sun, like each well-known individual within the galaxy, can be in assessment to a massive nuclear reactor. Deep within the Sun's middle, nuclear fusion reactions produce massive portions of power that radiates from the Sun's floor and into place inside the shape of slight strength and heat.

Solar radiation may be transformed into thermal energy (warmness) or electric powered strength.

In this ebook we are able to mainly hobby on using solar strength for strength technology.

Solar radiation may be transformed immediately into electricity by way of way of gadgets known as solar cells (furthermore referred to as photovoltaic cells) via a mechanism wherein the effect of slight with the junction amongst a metal and a semiconductor (including silicon) generates a very small electrical voltage. The strength generated thru a unmarried photovoltaic cell is usually very small, approximately watts. However, with the aid of manner of connecting a couple of cells to shape modules, and a couple of modules to every specific to shape photovoltaic panels, it's far viable to generate hundreds or maybe masses of kilowatts of power.

STRENGTHS OF SOLAR ENERGY

•The maximum crucial energy of sun electricity is that it's miles a renewable energy supply. Solar electricity may be harnessed in all regions of the sector and is available every day. In addition, now not like fossil fuels, sun energy is a in reality inexhaustible deliver of electricity this is constantly handy for the following five-7 billion years, this is till the solar collapses, consistent with scientists.

•Solar power can be used for numerous capabilities. With it, it's miles possible to generate each power, via photovoltaic systems, and warmth thru thermal flora. It may be critical for producing energy in regions with out get right of access to to the electricity grid, for water distillation in arid regions of developing global places, or even for powering satellites in location.

•Solar power allows you to generate strength on your very personal to fulfill element or perhaps all of your strength dreams. Obviously this could have a proper away effect at the price of your energy bills, which you could see reduced dramatically proper away. The financial savings to your bill will rely on the scale of the sun system and your electricity or warm temperature intake.

•Solar systems commonly have a median life of more than 30 years and do now not require lots preservation. The first-rate crucial renovation way can be to preserve them as smooth as feasible; generally washing the panels is completed multiple instances a 12 months.

Therefore, after defensive the initial charge of the solar device, there may be little or no rate for preservation and repair art work.

•Finally, a energy that should no longer be underestimated is that a era in sun energy is constantly evolving and enhancements will accentuate within the future. New discoveries and resulting improvements inside the regions of quantum physics and nanotechnology have the capacity to boom the effectiveness of sun panels to double or perhaps triple their performance.

WEAKNESSES OF SOLAR ENERGY

•There isn't any hiding the truth that the initial rate of purchasing a sun device is quite excessive. You will should cope proper now with procuring sun panels, inverters, batteries and, if you aren't in charge of it, additionally for technicians to take care of the installation. Nevertheless, those types of technologies are continuously growing and call for is

4

continuously increasing, so it is stable to expect that charges will most probable come down in the destiny.

•Although solar electricity can still be collected inside the direction of cloudy and rainy days, without a shadow of a doubt the overall performance of the sun tool decreases. In addition, one need to moreover do not forget that sun strength can not be gathered at some stage in the night time. To overcome this trouble, a battery device need to be hooked up, which, lamentably, is form of typically rather cumbersome and steeply-priced.

•The more strength you need to supply, the greater solar panels you will want to build up as lots daytime as viable. Even so, solar panels require an entire lot of location, and now not all roofs are large sufficient to keep the right large kind of sun panels to fulfill your power goals.

•Solar power also has a trustworthy amount of environmental effect and is responsible for diverse varieties of pollution. This stems from the discharge of poisonous substances and perilous merchandise used all through the producing process of solar photovoltaic systems, that can't immediately have an effect on the surroundings. In addition, each the transportation and set up of solar panels result in the emission of greenhouse gases. Despite this, sun power continues to be a renewable and comparatively easy deliver that during no way, from an environmental component of view, can be in comparison to fossil fuels.

STAND-ALONE SOLAR SYSTEMS (OFF-GRID)

Off-grid sun structures, also called stand-on my own solar structures, have the peculiarity of now not being associated with the power grid and, therefore, are definitely autonomous. As is the case with on-grid structures, this form of solar panel generates extra energy than it consumes, however instead of feeding extra power again into the grid, it stores it in batteries making sure that it's far always available at diverse times of the day, mainly inside the path of the vain nights.

One of the primary capabilities of off-grid sun electricity structures is that because of the fact they are disconnected from the strength grid, they are now not affected the least bit through any strength outages, continuing to perform even inside the occasion of failures in the electricity grid.

Off-grid solar systems are exceptional for all customers who, due to the geographical location in which they stay, can not consequences connect with the power grid.

The number one advantage of this form of tool is to turn out to be electricity self-enough, having fixed electricity charges and no payments.

Another thrilling trouble of off-grid structures is that they're modular, this means that that they may be modular and will let you growth the capability of your device as your electricity dreams grow. Ideally, you have to start with a small device after which, through the years, increase its length.

In most instances, however, off-grid sun installations want to be blended with the use of strength mills, as a way to be able to offer strength generation inside the direction of periods of immoderate call for or even as weather situations are unfavourable. For example, in wintry climate at immoderate latitudes there's much less availability of daylight hours and heavy snowfall can purpose panels to be partly or surely included.

WHY CHOOSE A STAND-ALONE SOLAR SYSTEM?

As said inside the preceding paragraphs, the maximum drastically used solar systems are on-grid structures, i.E., the ones linked to the electricity grid, and this is largely due to reasons. The first reason is only financial in nature in that an off-grid solar machine can also moreover furthermore have better set up costs than a traditional tool. The second reason, rather, is of a sensible nature and stems from the viable troubles that a "non-technical man or woman" would possibly come across at some point of the installation method of the machine.

So why want to you choose an off-grid solar device?

The answer is quite simple: the advantages of this form of device a ways outweigh the terrible components each for folks who wanted to use it as a supply of power for their domestic and for folks that desired an impartial supply of energy for a so-known as "amusement" manner of transportation, with unique reference to campers and caravans.

STAND-ALONE SOLAR SYSTEMS FOR RESIDENTIAL USE

Without a shadow of a doubt, on-grid, i.E., grid-associated, solar energy systems are, so far, the maximum famous and big inside the houses of these who have determined to apply solar energy to supply the energy had to preserve their homes.

Although at the start appearance this may appear like a fee-powerful solution, customers of conventional solar systems brief come to phrases with the marketplace price of strength. Regardless of processes it's far produced, power is paid at expenses starting from 3 to 10 cents/kWh, with a median reference price (the so-referred to as PUN) of about five cents/kWh.

With one of these promoting charge, for there to be a actual cross lower back, power might must be produced thru very huge flora that control to cut down on set up and working fees and therefore resemble power flora more than residential sun panels.

To date, a PV tool for residential use therefore is available specifically for people who need to apply it for self-consumption thru an off-grid gadget that includes the usage of batteries that could preserve the greater strength produced in the end of the day and that may be drawn on when there may be no availability of daytime.

the installation of this shape of sun tool has numerous blessings. Let's go through the principle ones:

•The largest advantage of using stand-on my own solar panels in your property is to mention goodbye for proper to all of the regular electricity costs which might be typically located for your software program bill. This is possible because of the truth with an off-grid machine there can be no need to spark off any supply contracts or agreements with electricity grid operators, collectively with e-distribution or the GSE.

•An off-grid solar device may be established in your home by means of manner of filing a easy graduation note to the municipality of wherein the belongings is placed. This does no longer examine to conventional structures, the set up of which requires greater office paintings and, therefore, more time to look your tool up and running. It ought to be said, however, that even for off-grid installations, exclusive regulations might also have a take a look at if the assets is located in historic facilities or regions of specific landscape interest.

In addition, even inside the event of destiny plant adjustments, along with relocation, growth, or alternative of modules or batteries, no new office work is probably required

•Finally, off-grid solar systems are first-class for set up in all the ones isolated dwellings (mountain inns, mountain huts) that cannot take advantage of the power produced through conventional solar structures due to the fact they're no longer located in city settings and, consequently, not able to connect to the countrywide strength grid.

STAND-ALONE SOLAR SYSTEMS FOR MOTORHOMES OR CARAVANS

As all RV or trailer owners will apprehend, having strength available at all times is vital for masses motives: the fridge, lighting fixtures, heating, and the functionality to price mobile phones, laptops, and distinct devices all rely upon a dependable supply of electricity.

Most RV and caravan electric powered systems run on 12-volt batteries, just like vehicle batteries but able to completing numerous hundred rate and discharge cycles. However,there may be numerous techniques to price those auxiliary batteries that during turn electricity your vehicle. One of these is solar energy via an off-grid device.

The set up of this form of solar system has severa advantages. Let's go through the primary ones:

•The largest gain of the usage of stand-by myself solar panels to your RV or trailer comes from the reality that, as soon as hooked up, they require little or no protection or individual motion to feature effectively. You will simplest want to connect the panels and connect them to the roof of your vehicle to have a dependable supply of strength for decades to head lower back, anyplace daylight may be to be had.

Most sun panels have a life expectancy of 25-30 years and are designed to face as plenty as many years of sun, rain, snow, hail, similarly to resist excessive wind speeds on highways.

All this isn't assured one-of-a-kind property of recharging, along side generators. These, in truth, require the acquisition of gasoline to function and require periodic safety of the entire line. In assessment, the best shape of renovation that solar panels need to go through is a clean cleansing simply so they always provide maximum output.

•An off-grid sun device allows you to pick out out a vast variety of locations (even an extended manner flung ones) wherein to camp, regardless of whether or now not grid connections are to be had. Also, for folks who were involved about walking out of power at some point of a barely a high-quality deal much less sunny day, that is not frequently a trouble as sun panels are in spite of the truth that capable of seize a number of the sun's rays, even in cloudy or in element shaded situations. A few hours of light are sufficient to absolutely charge most RV and caravan batteries so that you are commonly absolutely self-sufficient for some of days with out the need to recharge batteries.

•Another benefit that need to not be underestimated is the region of solar panels on your vehicle. They are generally mounted on the roof of RVs or trailers to maximize publicity to daytime, but this additionally permits you to free up precious vicinity inner that would in any other case want to be occupied via a generator.

There are forms of shocks you can get - the number one form of marvel is the surprise you get at the identical time as you are to be had direct touch with strength, and the alternative is the type of marvel you get when you have a take a look at your month-to-month electricity bill! Recently, it looks like more and more people are receiving that 2d form of wonder - human beings whinge approximately their ever-growing power payments despite the fact that they may be superb that they have now not prolonged their power consumption. Increased strength bills can be a prime setback for people who are looking to maintain cash or who are having a tough time making ends meet. In this monetary smash we're going to take a deeper take a look at out this trouble and parent out what truly is occurring to your electricity payments, and why it is going on now.

Identify the Problem

The first aspect which you want to do is to find out how a whole lot your invoice has prolonged with the resource of. Knowing this quantity will help you to apprehend the trouble and get a higher perception into the adjustments that have happened. To do that all you need to do is check your vintage electricity payments. Use the vintage bills to discover what number of devices of electricity you've got were given used each month in the beyond, and notice if there can be a consistent growth from month to month or a lovely spike.

A sudden spike in your energy bill might be the stop give up result of a few new digital tool that you latterly supplied. It is also viable that the charge in line with unit has progressed - examine how a bargain your strength organisation charged in step with unit within the past, whilst the payments have been affordable, with the amount that they may be charging now. This is in particular probable if you have these days modified your electricity dealer or have moved homes - your new provider can also have a higher rate in step with unit.

There are different occurrences that could offer an reason behind a spike in your energy bill:

Firstly, your power dealer ought to have prolonged the expenses in step with unit, or the government may also want to have raised the costs or taxes. It is crucial to stay updated on these items in case you want to preserve your self from pulling your hair searching out the motive why your strength invoice has suddenly long long past up.

The second state of affairs that could account for an sudden spike to your energy bill could be your tariff. When you circulate house or trade your power provider, you typically get a trendy tariff with low charges. However, after a 12 month duration, the carriers roll you over to their amazing quotes which are very steeply-priced. This may additionally want to offer an reason for why after months of your power invoice being at a notable rate factor, it has suddenly jumped to a trendy high.

To make sure that you in no manner get overcharged, it's far recommended that you take your meter readings your self and take a look at them with the ones on the bill to make certain that every one of the statistics is correct. A final reason for being overcharged to hold in thoughts is probably a damaged meter. Though strength groups usually make certain that this doesn't display up, and speedy restore the broken meters, it isn't absolutely no longer viable.

To see whether or not or no longer your meter is damaged or not, you need to close the power to your property truly. A phrase of caution - do not try this with the useful resource of switching off all of your lighting fixtures and home equipment! Instead, flip off the precept strength button after which look at the meter to look if it's far however strolling. It must no longer be displaying any power utilization in any respect. If you notice that the meter is still going for walks even irrespective of the entirety power to the residence has been close off, the meter is damaged and leaking electricity that lets in you to motive the growth on your payments.

Accurate Billing vs. Estimated Billing

The device of billing which you use is a few special important difficulty that affects the power bills. The accurate billing device is the normal one, in which the strength dealer installs a meter at the customer's house, and the billed amount is ready right now at the energy used. In an anticipated billing device, the electricity supply industrial organization employer generates the electrical bill based on an estimate of ways an entire lot power the circle of relatives makes use of. In expected billing, it does now not simply rely how loads strength is virtually fed on - you could be some distance from home for a month and though get charged as a amazing deal as you commonly do. In assessment, in case your enterprise follows an energetic billing tool you may best be charged for some thing little home power use which you used inside the path of your holiday.

It's additionally definitely really worth thinking about that the unexpected upward push in your electricity payments also can be attributed to a cutting-edge switch among those billing structures. It is more commonplace to get preserve of higher bills at the same time as you turn from an expected billing tool to an correct billing one, however the opposite may also moreover display up.

Affect of the Size of the House on Energy Costs

It's moreover very crucial to consider that shifting to a bigger house will bring about higher strength bills. If there are more rooms that want lighting or home equipment that require strength, then manifestly the bills might be better. Generally, smaller sized homes do now not get very excessive payments as the overall power necessities are usually decrease than the necessities of big homes.

Saving Money in your Energy Bill

One of the situations above should have defined the sudden spike that you've seen in your strength invoice. The question now will be: How are you capable of maintain extra in your electricity bill? The manner to this query is what this e-book is all approximately. Even in case you are properly-to-do and might effects pay the bills, the training in this ebook can however assist you - notwithstanding the entirety, aren't there topics which might be more a laugh to invest in than electricity? In the following chapters, we're going to cognizance on strategies that you may use to decrease your bills and begin saving. The benefits of these modifications aren't surely economic, each! The a good deal a good deal much less electricity you use, the extra blessings you make contributions to the environment and the monetary system. Our society wastes masses of strength without identifying it, and thinking about we rely intently on non-renewable energy property we are contributing to their depletion. Research has discovered that the strength consumption in America has been developing each yr, and doubles every 20 years.

There's a commonplace false impression that saving energy technique which you want to take a seat in darkish rooms with the lights off. That's not true! Instead, saving energy is ready easy adjustments like the usage of electricity-green domestic gadget that do the job truely as well but keep energy rather than losing it. There are many things that you may do to hold the surroundings green (and positioned some greater inexperienced in your wallet), whilst saving a massive amount in your bills. Some of those strategies encompass:

- Using power-efficient home equipment
- Going green
- Using renewable and sustainable power anywhere viable

Each of the following chapters can be centered on precise strategies, strategies, and subjects for you to offer you with recommendations, and suggestions to maintain on your energy bills in an easy and renewable way.

Chapter 2: Principles Of Electrical Engineering

Before addressing in element how a photovoltaic machine is made and the way it's miles set up, it's miles important to enunciate a few smooth standards concerning electric engineering , this is, the world that research the manufacturing, transmission and distribution of strength.

But do not worry! I may not bore you with prolonged and complicated physics formulation. The purpose of this bankruptcy is only that will help you understand the rudiments of the workings of electrical structures and the number one devices of length you may want to narrate to whilst you purchase all of the components of your sun tool.

ELECTRICITY AND POWER

Electricity is all round us: it powers the era of our each day lives which encompass cellular telephones, computer structures, lights systems or air conditioners, and it is observed in natural phenomena which incorporates lightning moves or synapses interior our brains. But what exactly is energy?

Electrical energy is usually defined because the go with the flow of electrical rate, that is, the movement of charged debris named electrons. In fashionable, electricity is the functionality to carry out artwork or observe a pressure to move an item. In the case of electrical strength, the pressure is the attraction or repulsion contemporary amongst charged particles. Electrical energy can be encountered in two paperwork: ability strength and kinetic power. However, we normally encounter electric powered powered power inside the form of functionality power, this is the electricity that is saved because of the relative characteristic of electrons, which may be not anything extra than the particles of which electric powered electricity is made. The motion of electrons thru an electric powered twine or exclusive medium is known as contemporary or power. There is likewise static electricity, which finally ends up from the imbalance or separation of great and horrific expenses on an item. Static strength is a form of electrical capability strength. If enough electric powered powered fee is gathered, the electrical capability electricity can be discharged to form a spark (or maybe lightning), or electric powered kinetic electricity.

LOOP

An electric powered powered powered circuit is a closed route wherein electric powered modern can glide.

An electrical circuit need to have a power deliver, wires thru which electricity can go with the flow, and a device together with a lamp or motor that uses the electric modern-day. All those components have to be connected simply so the present day flows continuously.

Small gadgets, which include a far flung manage or a flashlight, are powered through battery. In evaluation, in homes along side houses or faculties, most gadgets are powered with the aid of the usage of energy furnished thru the public strength plant.

Metal and plastic-included cables bring power spherical a circuit. Metal is a top notch conductor of electricity, which means that it could effortlessly go together with the waft alongside the cord. The plastic throughout the wire insulates the electricity and includes it just so it does now not damage human beings or different gadgets.

Finally, most circuits have a switch just so they will be have become on or off. Turning off the transfer reasons the circuit to open inflicting the go along with the glide of electrical modern-day-day to stop. Turning the turn on, however, motives the circuit to shut permitting the flow of electrical modern-day another time and, consequently, the operation of our tool.

That stated, we are able to say that each circuit will feature:

•Active additives (or turbines): that is, all the ones devices which is probably capable of presenting power to the circuit. The most common example of an active element is the stack.

•Passive components: in contrast, are all the ones gadgets that devour or maintain energy. Examples of passive additives are items along side slight bulbs or capacitors.

ALTERNATING CURRENT AND DIRECT CURRENT

Just like an ocean present day shifting in a specific course, energy additionally makes unique actions inner electric powered powered wires. Specifically, there are sorts of currents known as alternating cutting-edge (AC) and direct modern (DC).

In direct present day circuits, electrons circulate in quality one direction, from awful (-) to tremendous (+). Direct cutting-edge is a consistent present day that flows constantly until the circuit is became off or the electricity supply runs out or stops producing strength.

In alternating current-day circuits, electrons do not really glide but constantly trade direction thru vibrating back and forth, from negative (-) to top notch (+) and from exceptional (+) to bad (-).

Solar panels produce direct modern-day-day: the sun shining at the panels stimulates the glide of electrons, growing a modern. Since those electrons constantly go along with the go with the flow inside the same path, the current is non-stop.

Because our houses run on alternating modern-day (AC), sun panels require using a device referred to as an inverter.

The inverter's function is to transform direct contemporary (DC) to alternating present day

(AC) so that it is able to be applied in houses or lower returned to the strength grid. We will skip into greater element in this challenge depend within the following chapters.

UNITS OF MEASUREMENT OF ELECTRICAL ENERGY

Understanding what a photovoltaic device is and the way to independently accumulate it requires statistics of the primary bodily portions and gadgets of length of energy.

But what's a bodily amount? And a unit of size?

A bodily amount is described because the assets of a frame or phenomenon that can be measured quantitatively and, therefore, can be expressed by way of using numerous.

A unit of measurement, but, is nothing more than a amount this is taken as a time period of evaluation for measuring si all portions of the equal species.

Despite the apparent complexity of these necessities, it's going to suffice for us to apprehend that the three foremost bodily quantities in energy are electric powered powered powered powered voltage (V), electric powered modern-day (I) and electric resistance (R).

Each of these physical portions has its private unit of size, so electric powered powered voltage (V) could be measured in volts, electric powered contemporary-day may be measured in amperes, and electric resistance in ohms.

Because electric powered powered modern is invisible and the tactics involved in electronics are regularly difficult to illustrate, severa virtual additives are represented with the aid of hydraulic equivalents. More truly, we find out it less complicated to recognize to consider electricity as water flowing thru a pipe. From this it follows that electric powered powered voltage can be in comparison to water pressure, electric powered powered modern is equal to drift charge, and resistance is equal to the width of the pipe.

VOLTAGE

Electric voltage (T), whose unit of measurement is volts (V), is defined because the distinction in electric functionality (d.O.P.) at points in vicinity, i.E., the power required to transport an electric powered powered powered rate from factor A to issue B of an electric powered powered circuit.

If we remember a water tank at a positive top above the floor with a water pipe branching off the lowest, the pressure current on the give up of the pipe can represent voltage. The water inside the tank represents the electric rate. The greater water there may be inside the reservoir, the more the electrical price and, therefore, the extra the stress measured on the surrender of the tube.

We can recall this reservoir as a battery in which we preserve a positive amount of power after which release it. If we discharge a high-quality amount of water from our tank, the strain created on the stop of the tube decreases. We can agree with this as a lower in voltage. This takes region, for example, at the same time as the mild emanating from a flashlight dims because the batteries are approximately to discharge.

The most rate of electrical voltage present inside the systems of commonplace houses, i.E., common circle of relatives stores, is 230

V. However, this determine can also variety depending on the place of the property at severa elements at the countrywide grid.

In addition, all additives in electric powered circuits have voltages measured in volts. For instance, an AA alkaline battery gives 1.Five volts and could exceptional be able to electricity components with the identical kind of volts.

The price of electrical voltage (or voltage), therefore, permits us to tell whether or not or no longer the numerous components of an electrical system are nicely ideal with each unique.

AMPERE-HOUR

Ampere-hour (Ah) is some different important unit of measurement that represents the amount of charge required to supply the modern of 1 ampere for one hour. It is therefore identical to 3600 coulombs and is particularly used to understand how lengthy a battery will run out (e.G., a 1 Ah battery continuously turning in 1 A will discharge in one hour, handing over 500 mA will discharge in 2 hours).

From a practical aspect of view, furthermore, the ampere-hour is important as it allows us to diploma the amount of energy a battery is capable of storing. For the same purpose, the kilowatt-hour (kWh), each different unit of size that we are capable of address later within the bankruptcy, will are available on hand.

Nevertheless, if you want to recognize the perfect duration of battery desired for our PV gadget, it is also crucial to keep in mind the price of the voltage at which it's far used: the higher the voltage, the decrease its potential in ampere-hours may be. For example, if a 24 kWh battery that is used at 12 V should have a potential of 2000 Ah, even as the same battery used at 24 V could have a capability this is exactly half of of that (one thousand Ah).

POWER

Power (P), whose unit of measurement is the watt (W), represents the price at which energy is produced or ate up. More mainly, watt is the unit of dimension that informs us how hundreds power is launched each 2d.

Returning to our analogy with hydraulic systems, the watt represents the power that would offer water flowing thru a pipe to show a mill wheel.

In electrical structures, the electricity is equal to the electric voltage prolonged by using way of way of the electric cutting-edge. If, as an instance, the electrical current is four A and the electric voltage is 220 v, multiplying the 2 elements will offer a energy of 880 w.

One would probable keep in mind watts as a degree that tells us how large the "flow" of electricity must be to make our electric device art work.

To use a realistic example, a 100 W bulb consumes strength at a better price than a 60 W bulb. This manner that the only hundred W bulb calls for extra "flux" to perform.

Similarly, the price at which your sun panel "flows" strength into your house is measured in watts.

Generally, the most famous family sun panels to be had within the market have electricity scores among 250 and four hundred watts. The term "rated" refers back to the strength rating at the nameplate and tells us the maximum energy our panel can be able to deliver at reference environmental conditions. This manner that, in truth, this price also can variety.

WATT-HOURS AND KILOWATT-HOURS

Although the watt is the usual worldwide unit for measuring power, family energy consumption is measured in watt-hours (Wh) or kilowatt-hours (kWh).

Watt-hour is the unit of size defined because the complete energy introduced if an electrical energy of 1 watt is maintained for one hour of time. It is equivalent to three,600 joules.

The kilowatt-hour, alternatively, is the unit of size similar to the general energy added if an electric powered powered power of one,000 watts is maintained for one hour of time. In this situation it is identical to a few,six hundred,000 joules.

It is crucial to become familiar with the latter unit of length as it's miles the handiest maximum generally used to diploma electricity consumption, in addition to being the first-rate indexed on energy bills.

PEAK POWER (WP)

Solar panel top power, the unit of it's watt-peak (Wp), is the maximum electric powered power that a solar panel machine is able to generating under the following famous conditions:

• Temperature: 20 levels Celsius

• Irradiance acquired: one thousand W/m²

• Air mass: 1.5

The air mass measures the distance traveled with the aid of solar radiation as it passes through the surroundings and varies with the mind-set of occurrence.

Irradiance is the electricity in step with unit vicinity of sun radiation incident at the floor of a solar cell. We will complex extra on this concept in the following chapters.

In photovoltaic panel statistics sheets, power is generally stated in watt-height in area of watt-hour, and this is supposed to emphasize to the customer that a solar panel (e.G., 70 watt-hour) will not produce the least bit hours of the day 70 watts of electricity each hour but the electricity generated can be variable and relying on the situations formerly said.

The notion of watt-top is used to examine the overall typical overall performance of solar photovoltaic structures and to are looking ahead to the amount of strength they may produce. The higher the watt-top (Wp) fee, for the equal ground area, the extra green the panel is probably.

Watt-peak, moreover, is used to calculate the size of a photovoltaic system primarily based on the quantity of power to be generated, considering daylight hours situations.

Different peak electricity is acquired from the identical sun panel relying at the place of the PV tool and its daylight conditions.

Therefore, on the roof of a house in Stockholm, a one kWp device will produce six hundred kilowatt hours (kWh) in step with three hundred and sixty five days, at the same time due to the fact the equal sun panel in an Italian residence will produce 1250 kWh/3 hundred and sixty 5 days.

RESISTANCE

Resistance, whose unit of measurement is the ohm (Ω), is a diploma of competition to modern-day float in an electrical circuit.

To better recognize the concept of resistance, permit us to once more resort to our analogy with hydraulic systems.

Consider two water tanks, considered considered one of which has a narrow pipe and the opportunity has a substantial pipe. If those are crossed via a waft of water, the narrow pipe will offer extra resistance to the go together with the glide passing through it despite the fact that the water has the identical stress as the tank with the broader pipe.

In electric terms, considering circuits with identical voltages and specific resistances, the circuit with the higher resistance will allow an entire lot much much less "go together with the go with the flow" of modern-day, on the identical time as the circuit with the higher resistance will permit less electric powered powered current to go together with the go with the flow through it.

All substances contemporary in nature offer a few degree of resistance to the go together with the glide of electrical cutting-edge-day.

They are outstanding into:

•Conductors: this is, those substances that offer little resistance to the glide of electrical present day. Examples embody metals which include gold, aluminum or copper, the latter being the maximum usually used in the production of electrical structures.

•Insulators: conversely, the ones substances that provide some degree of resistance to the go with the flow of electrical current. Examples are materials collectively with plastic, wood or rubber.

The electric resistance values of the numerous additives of a circuit (together with a resistor can be) are normally given in reference manuals or at the nameplate of the issue.

In order for the popularity of a selected element or the whole circuit to be showed, extemporaneous measurements of electrical resistance may be made. This lets in us to come across feasible damage to conductors (which includes burning or corrosion) if the electric resistance charge is surprisingly high. Conversely, if the electrical resistance fee is abnormally low, this can be due to damage to the insulators precipitated, for instance, through overheating or moisture.

OHM'S LAW AND THE RELATIONSHIP BETWEEN VOLTS, AMPS AND WATTS

Having addressed the main physical portions that come into play in electric powered phenomena, it's time to region it all collectively and close the loop.

Combining the elements of voltage, contemporary and resistance, physicist Georg Ohm developed the system:

$V = I \times R$

That is, the electric voltage is identical to the electrical modern-day increased thru the charge of the electric resistance.

This components is known as Ohm's regulation.

Although for the purpose of the ebook it may seem superfluous to talk about uninteresting physical components, Ohm's law will are available in to be had often from a realistic element of view. This is due to the fact the overall electric powered resistance of an electrical circuit (with its various components) isn't always usually straight away measurable.

Engineers, therefore, treasure Ohm's law with the beneficial aid of deriving circuit resistance from voltage and contemporary:

R = V / I

Similarly, knowledge the charge of voltage and resistance, it is viable to calculate the electric current:

I = V / R

Another physical technique this is very useful from a sensible trouble of view is one which relates voltage, current and power.

To wit:

V = P / I

For instance, if we've a one hundred W motor with a five A modern-day-day, it's going to run at 20 V

Similarly, understanding the rate of the electricity and voltage, it is possible to calculate the electrical present day:

I = P / V

Thus, a one hundred W motor powered at 20 V calls for a 5 A contemporary.

CONNECTIONS IN THE CIRCUITS

Very regularly numerous passive factors (users), which embody moderate bulbs or resistors, or numerous energetic factors (generators), most often represented with the useful aid of batteries, are inserted within the identical circuit.

Users and generators may be related in three terrific strategies: collection, parallel, or series-parallel.

Two or greater customers are connected in series at the same time as they are inserted into the circuit one after the opportunity virtually so they'll be handed thru successively with the aid of way of the same electric powered present day-day. This reasons the operation of each client to depend upon the handiest in advance than it.

A fashionable realistic example of collection clients is the relationship of slight bulbs inside the Christmas tree: if truly certainly one of them is electrocuted, all the others will continue to be unlit.

The voltage that permits the bulbs to be grew to become on is the sum of the voltages required to turn at the man or woman bulbs.

Thus, three 2 V bulbs associated in collection can be capable of be lit via a 6 V battery. A decrease battery voltage will purpose the bulbs to expose on little or now not anything, while a higher voltage might be disproportionate and could purpose them to burn out. As for the complete resistance, it'll be identical to the sum of the individual resistances.

Two or greater clients, instead, are related in parallel if they have the results in commonplace-this is, the input and output of current-day. This causes them to be associated with the generator independently, with two or more alternative paths for the waft of electrical cutting-edge-day-day.

Therefore, if one of the users were to fail, the operation of the others should not be affected. In exclusive terms, if one bulb burns out, all of the others hold to function.

However, in this example, all the bulbs will want to have an same flip-on voltage due to the fact the generator (stack). Nevertheless, every bulb can also draw a distinctive contemporary due to the fact the generator will provide a whole contemporary equal to the sum of the currents drawn with the beneficial resource of the person bulbs. As for the overall resistance, it'll continuously be lots plenty much less than the man or woman resistors connected.

As for the lively elements, i.E., generators, they may be stated to be connected in series even as the extremely good pole of 1 is hooked up to the terrible pole of the alternative, and so on till the so-referred to as battery of batteries is shaped.

The voltage of a battery of batteries related in collection can be identical to the sum of the person voltages; the current, rather, may be same to that which a unmarried battery must supply. The usefulness of connecting multiple turbines in series emerges whilst, for the operation of the customers in a given circuit, a better voltage than a unmarried battery is to be exploited.

Two or more turbines, but, are said to be related in parallel even as all of the horrific poles and all of the high-quality poles of the man or woman stacks are joined together, respectively, which need to always be equal.

The voltage of a battery of batteries related in parallel might be same to that of a single battery, whilst the cutting-edge it could deliver can be same to the sum of the currents of the man or woman batteries.

There are circuits wherein some components, whether or not or no longer lively or passive, are linked in series at the equal time as others are linked in parallel. Such circuits are known as series-parallel circuits. Since the ones forms of circuits are a combination of every modes of connection, to calculate the values of voltage, present day-day and resistance, it will likely be vital to find out the quantities of the circuit related in series and those connected in parallel and exercising the pointers we've got were given positioned out as though they have been unbiased circuits.

HOW ASTRONOMICAL DISTANCES ARE CALCULATED

To calculate astronomical distances, the brightness, rate and orbit of the celestial our bodies must be taken beneath attention.

Within one hundred moderate-years from Earth, the triangulation approach is used. Up to 10 thousand moderate-years, electromagnetic radiation spectrum assessment is used.

Triangulation

The triangulation approach is based totally on the principle of trigonometry.

According to this precept, it's far possible to calculate, via facts of one issue and one attitude of the rectangle, all the factors of a triangle.

So it's far enough to bring together a triangle with a movie star vertex to recognise the suitable distance of the latter.

The base corresponds to the road turning into a member of the two contrary factors of the Earth's orbit.

The ellipse this is seen from Earth under a brilliant mind-set, that's measured with the sextant, is used to calculate the attitude on the vertex.

Finally, the angle is halved, the tangent is calculated, and the semi-crucial axis of the Earth orbit is divided thru the tangent of the perspective.

The spectrum approach for calculating astronomical distances

As we've already noted, the spectrum technique is used to degree celestial our bodies up to ten thousand mild-years away.

With this technique, we analyze the spectrum of electromagnetic radiation: this is, we look at the set of moderate waves we see coming from the movie star.

Indeed, we're capable of determine how a long manner away a given object is through way of knowing absolutely the brightness and intensity of slight we see and measuring the lower in brightness.

CEPHEIDS

When we want to move beyond our galaxy, we hotel to the Cepheid method.

These are stars that pulsate like fireflies, at some point of the galaxies.

In this situation, the time among one and the alternative of maximum brightness is evaluated.

It is a consistent time, however it varies from movie star to famous individual: the longer it's miles, the greater the brightness.

By measuring the length of a Cepheid, you may still with out issues discern out its actual brightness, which, in assessment to its apparent brightness, additionally offers the distance.

"Astronomical unit" is used to express astronomical distances

The astronomical unit is a unit of size used usually inside the Solar System.

As of 2012 it's miles defined through an appropriate charge 149 597 870 seven hundred meters, which is prepared the space most of the Sun and Earth.

The first rate image for astronomical unit is AU (short for astronomical unit), however the image UA, applied in Italian-language texts, is likewise usually everyday.

We will now offer an reason of in element the definition of the latter and word a way to transform astronomical gadgets to other devices, every astronomical and nonastronomical.

In specific, we're able to speak a manner to transfer from astronomical units to moderate-365 days, parsec and specific I.S. (International System) devices of measurement, which includes kilometer.

THE ASTRONOMICAL UNIT

As said above, the astronomical unit is applied in Astronomy and corresponds to the distance amongst Earth and the Sun.

At the twenty 8th General Assembly of the International Astronomical Union that turned into held in 2012, it changed into determined through definition that 1 astronomical unit (1 AU) corresponds exactly to 149 597 870 seven-hundred meters:

now you will be thinking why we communicate about common distance and now not, more genuinely, the distance between Earth and the Sun.

The motivation is sort of simple, the Earth has an 'elliptical orbit and sooner or later of its movement of revolution holds various distances from the Sun.

Specifically, we realise from Kepler's first regulation that the Earth inside the route of its movement of revolution describes an ellipse of which the Sun occupies one of the foci. Two factors are especially critical in this specific motion:

1) perihelion, this is the issue of shortest distance at which the Sun is ready 147.1 million km far from Earth

2) aphelion, the aspect of most distance in which the Sun and Earth are at a distance of 100 and fifty- million kilometers.

By mathematics averaging the cost of 149.6 million km among those two distances, this common can be approximated to an appropriate charge of 1 astronomical unit.

Chapter 3: How To Perform Your Calculations For A System

When we speak approximately calculating a sun set up we imply the fee-gain ratio , financing alternatives and the use of government subsidies.

This consists of compensation for introduced strength generated.

Added to this are the economic savings over the use of traditional power assets.

All those gadgets want to be evaluated properly earlier.

This is the handiest manner to calculate whether or now not or not an installation is appropriate for sun electricity production and whether or no longer it actually can pay off in character instances.

What belongs to the solar machine ?

First, it have to be pointed out that the sun presents electricity without spending a dime.

It shines in the sky, is amassed with the resource of solar panels on the roof and saved in an accumulator.

The family uses a photovoltaic tool to produce, which moreover they use at domestic.

For this to be feasible, the proper technology is needed, which includes no longer best solar collector stores.

More technical system is wanted with which sunlight hours may be used.

All this actually prices a number of cash.

But there can be moreover profits because of the reality the electricity produced through the PV device can be fed into the general public power grid.

For this, the family gets a small price.

In maximum instances , solar rooftop structures produce masses extra energy than the circle of relatives consumes.

Therefore, these income have a difficult and rapid length , which have to be considered in the calculation.

But because intake is extraordinary in every family due to the truth the charges of the PV system are very notable, it's miles important to apply a so-called PV yield calculator.

You can locate it on the Internet thru a are looking for engine.

With this kind of calculator , you may find out in a few terms what the fee-advantage ratio is.

HOW TO CALCULATE THE CORRECT ANGLE FOR SOLAR PANELS IN SOLAR PHOTOVOLTAIC SYSTEM

To get the maximum out of solar panels , you want to component the solar panel in the path that captures the most sunlight hours.

Knowing the manner to calculate the best mind-set for solar panels will help you get the most out of them.

If you live within the northern hemisphere, you want to orient the panels within the course of the south.

If you live within the southern hemisphere, your panels have to face north.

Most owners of sun power structures mount the panels in a tough and speedy position , in which the panels may be tilted manually as wished.

Here are some techniques to calculate the exquisite mindset for sun panels:

Method 1: brief and smooth

Subtract 15 ranges for summer season and add 15 ranges for wintry climate at your range.

For example: if the latitude is forty stages, the perspective you want to tilt the panels in wintry weather is: 40 + 15 = fifty 5 levels

In summer time, however, it is probably: 40-15 = 25 tiers.

Method 2 : for the cold season

In the wintry weather months, at the same time as there can be a great deal much less sunlight hours you handiest need to multiply your range via 0.Nine and upload 29 stages.

So if the range is forty ranges, the angle to be tilted in wintry weather is:

(forty * zero.Nine) + 29 = sixty 5 levels.

This technique is an entire lot extra profitable than the previous, because the panels are already became closer to sunlight hours in the center of the day on brief wintry weather days.

Method three : for respectable season

This time you may must multiply your range thru the use of zero.Nine and subtract 23.Five levels.

So if your variety is forty degrees, the panels need to be tilted through: (40 * zero.Nine) - 23.Five = 12.Five ranges.

Method 4: for spring and autumn

From your range without a doubt subtract 2.Five tiers.

So if your range is forty degrees, the great tilt for the panels in spring and fall may be: 40 - 2.Five = 37.Five degrees.

If you discover that the power generated with the useful resource of your panels is enough for your iciness strength goals-due to the fact your most power intake is in the wintry climate-you could sincerely go away the panels in the identical place.

Of route you may observe that consistent-mount sun panels can be tons much less powerful in the course of summer time, spring and fall , due to the fact the sun moves in the course of an lousy lot of the sky.

Panel systems that "song" the sun's feature are greater green, but additionally extra pricey.

Obviously the right perspective for solar panels is the proper location, however inside the actual worldwide we cope with bushes and homes that can encompass the panels or areas with masses of leaves, dust or debris.

It may be critical to modify the attitude barely to compensate for a far much less than tremendous charge.

Knowing the manner to calculate the nice perspective for solar panels will assist you generate more power out of your solar energy device.

Fortunately, there can be a device called a solar tracker as a way to automatically orient sun panels closer to the solar to maximise their universal performance.

Although it's far an additional investment , a few human beings might also additionally moreover locate that the prolonged performance is properly worth the additional cost.

One some of the numerous questions we ask is a way to calculate the output of each panel.

How loads strength are we able to produce a from a energy plant at some degree inside the yr?

How a super deal for inside the destiny?

More importantly, how an entire lot do I want to growth my home from an energy perspective?

It isn't clean to offer an answer to this question however now we are able to try to answer it really.

First, it need to be specific that there are numerous elements on which manufacturing is primarily based upon.

One has to recollect viable intermittent shading that would have an effect at the solar panels at some point of daylight.

You must ask whether or not or now not or now not your plant gets enough moderate and six your solar panels are massive sufficient.

Both seasons and weather conditions have a exceptional impact and decide the amount of sunlight absorbed through the PV device.

Solar energy peaks in June, July and even August.

During this era, any 3-kwp power plant can produce up to six hundred kilowatts and 200 kilowatts in January.

WHAT POWER AM I USING?

The kilowatt-hour, kWh, is the primary unit of power.

Electricity bills show the not unusual form of kWh inside the direction of the month.

The not unusual intake of a circle of relatives of four is amongst 3500 and 4000 Kwh in line with twelve months, this price varies drastically.

Simply take the bills for the beyond three hundred and sixty five days and the power ate up.

Divide your common month-to-month utilization with the resource of 30 and get your commonplace each day usage.

Calculate that during summer time, at least in Italy, there may be the height of consumption, because of air conditioners.

If you want to get an concept of the not unusual in Italy, take a look at the statistics.

HOW MANY PHOTOVOLTAIC PANELS DO I NEED

Typically, a PV module produces amongst 250 and 350 peak energy under high-quality situations.

Thus, for a three Kwp device, about 10 panels are usually used.

Photovoltaic panels produce direct current , while we need alternating present day.

The artwork of transformation is the challenge of the inverter, a tool that is constantly discovered in systems.

There is a "loss" within the conversion amongst direct present day and alternating present day-day-day.

This way that when you convert approximately 80% of CC, you turn to CA.

But losses are inevitable...

because of physics .

So if we've got a 6kW machine, we divide with the aid of 0.Eight.

This technique that 30 modules of 250 Wp or 270 Wp can be desired.

So how a extremely good deal can you shop to your power invoice?

Finally, allow's discover how hundreds you can shop for your software program invoice consistent with month.

On the Internet we're able to make a sufficient calculation of a plant's output via way of offering the coordinates of its location.

However, regardless of the truth that they may be approximate, we perform the calculations for you.

In essential Italy, each KWP of strength produces 1300 kilowatts of energy in keeping with one year.

In northern Italy 1200, in southern Italy even 1500

PHOTOVOLTAIC SYSTEMS AND HOW TO OPTIMIZE SOLAR ENERGY PRODUCTION

Depending on the ability and location of photovoltaic structures, they provide ecological strength to entire areas in the course of the day.

To gather this goal, systems have to characteristic perfectly, with a high diploma of performance, accessibility and profitability.

This is why the use of sensors is absolutely important at some elements in the approach chain.

And with the proper tool, the sun shines every day.

In addition to the fact that photovoltaic structures should produce as masses electricity as feasible, for the motive that maximum expensive strength flowers are frequently placed near the equator, and far from civilization, it is understood that any additives set up in the device should feature without failure for long periods of time.

This is in which SICK sensors are to be had , famend for his or her precise measurements and stability , as well as lengthy issuer existence.

In precise, the SICK Remote Service software program software is an financial and first rate promise.

It no longer simplest consists of activation and debugging jobs, but additionally gives one-time far flung aid

Fully bendy, SICK specialists are immediately at the press of a mouse , via cloud answers consistent with very strict protection standards.

The aggregate of clever sensors, fast issuer, and data network reduces the fee and additionally the performance of the set up- from the solar cell to the warm temperature exchanger thru the gas-fired emergency strength plant.

In addition, the Web-based issuer platform significantly reduces the making plans and configuration time for on-web net page issuer that can be desired.

SOLAR MONITORING FOR BETTER PERFORMANCE OF PHOTOVOLTAIC SYSTEMS

In heliostats, concentrators and solar modules a photovoltaic array, reflectors and sun cells are aligned with the solar all day lengthy.

For this, first , sensors are used to degree the tilt or rotation of reflectors and sun panels in a unmarried or dimensions, without touch.

Like real outdoor specialists, the sensors paintings on warm, bloodless, dusty or wet days.

Their digital thing can be very long lasting.

Using encoders to degree function; reflectors can precisely cognizance light at the sun that makes use of its energy.

Due to focused solar thermal electricity , hundreds of reflectors gather sun radiation on an absorbing floor.

At this focal point, molten salt or oil heats up and then flows thru pipes into heat accumulators or right away into the electricity plant.

Here are a number of the functions to maintain in thoughts whilst choosing a price controller.

First of all, environmental conditions have to be considered : if the installation situations of the controller are particularly extreme, the said walking temperature range need to be taken under attention.

Then the electric performance needs to be considered; it's miles recommended to take a look at the voltage panel with the PV generator coupling panel to make certain they'll be accurate;

Check that the most generator enter contemporary and maximum load functionality do no longer exceed the device present day, and take a look at the self-consumption in a unmarried-of-a-kind running situations.

HOW TO CHOOSE THE SOLAR THERMAL SYSTEM

In a sun thermal system , energy is transferred from daylight hours to water thru a panel at the roof of the house, a closed water loop , a water storage tank.

Here are some suggestions for figuring out which one is right for you.

There are styles of structures : motion and compelled flow into.

The former is much less tough to install and is pricey because of the fact the tank is above the panels and has significant leakage.

The second has a higher cost, however financial savings standard performance and allows more warmness water.

The tank can be established anywhere.

Let's observe them in element.

NATURAL CIRCULATION SYSTEM

Ideal for the latest water goals of a own family of four maximum: you could preserve 56% to 70% to your invoice every year

The purchase and set up fees are affordable.

It has a massive aesthetic effect on the roof on which the tank is mounted.

There it has extra heat loss however notwithstanding the truth that allows for desirable power conversion.

FORCED CIRCULATION SYSTEM

Compared with herbal move , it costs more and calls for specific location to area the tank.

However, it lets in for extra warm water production, a bigger own family, and extra financial financial savings on the software bill.

It converts sun electricity optimally and can be seamlessly protected with other devices.

SOLAR THERMAL

There are styles of solar thermal structures , the natural circulate system and the pressured glide system.

They produce domestic warm water through a place on the roof of the house that transfers the solar at once to the water via a tank and a closed hydraulic circuit.

But how does it paintings?

Water from the kettle can be used for all family uses : from showering to food guidance.

In addition, inside the maximum inexperienced houses, it can also be used for all domestic device that use electricity to supply warmth water, which includes washing machines and dishwashers.

In this way we additionally avoid electricity intake via the usage of water heated by means of the solar.

WHAT IS THE BEST SOLAR THERMAL SYSTEM?

We introduced stream and forced circulate structures to the laboratory.

But no longer all of them passed our exams.

Here are the results

If you're thinking about buying a solar thermal device, do not forget first:

The sizable form of humans in the house;

The opportunity of putting in the tank;

How an awful lot you can spend;

Integration with put up-heating with boiler.

There are specific very crucial elements to preserve in mind earlier than shopping for a sun thermal machine:

the house and the location in that you live,

the kind of panels you need and the economic savings and intake of 'strength.

Let's have a examine them in detail.

ACCOMODATION

Where do you stay?

Solar irradiance varies from area to location: in and on the coasts, for example, it's far extra than in the north.

Already at the layout degree, the vicinity in which you stay must be considered as a manner to choose out sun thermal panels which can make the maximum of the sun to deliver warmness water.

Therefore, one must carefully observe the thermal situations the climatic variations of the area wherein one lives.

Other elements to evaluate are the orientation of the roof and the size of your house: the suitable roof for solar thermal installation is going via south and with a 30-45°C pitch, whilst to calculate the dimensions of the machine it's far vital to recognize what's to be had inside the residence.

In fact, in addition to the panels, a boiler is also wanted wherein the water is contained to warm temperature.

Its capability glaringly is based upon on the form of collector

What approximately the sort of panels to be installation?

It essentially is based upon on two factors: the range of people residing in the residence and the every day dreams of each inhabitant of the residence.

TYPE OF PANELS

There are fundamental sorts of sun thermal panels

Flat-glass sun panels: collectively with glass to the sun however opaque to infrared rays, they will be bluette, a color that attracts the sun's rays most as it has the same frequency as them.

There can be a garage tank near the interior of the house, specifically in less heat locations.

Tubular vacuum panels: these are customary and characteristic notable ordinary performance and efficiency that may outperform flat panels by means of the use of the use of 15 to 20 percentage, specially in wintry weather.

It is possible to install them even in less warm climates because of actual standard performance at low solar radiation and coffee out of doors temperatures, they include a further fee.

The piping device, usually manufactured from copper, incorporates the heated water.

SAVING AND ENERGY CONSUMPTION

The project of sun panels is to capture the strength from the sun's rays and move returned it for exchange genuinely so the gadget can use it for boiler water.

The important benefit of this device is that thanks to the artwork finished with the resource of the sun thermal panel you're capable of keep away from the usage of the strength coming from the combustion of diesel gas, and the energy coming from the electricity grid with big fee economic financial savings in terms of manufacturing heat within the domestic.

This gadget also contributes to environmental sustainability thru the decreased use of fossil assets in select of renewables and the bargain of pollutant emissions.

If you're asking yourself any questions, we can answer them right away:

Will I actually have warm water all 12 months spherical?

You might also have warm water all three hundred and sixty five days spherical and extra than six months of the twelve months-it's far going to be heated through the solar.

During the autumn and wintry weather seasons, the sun will help to warmth it as lots as possible, supplementing the important strength wherein it's far desired with an electric heater or pre-present traditional boiler/water heater, even better with a warm temperature pump.

Experience from numerous installations confirms the opportunity of expertise big and consistent savings with a move again on funding of half the beneficial life.

However, the benefit of putting in this type of tool is confident, additionally it is carried out by using the use of a amazing style dressmaker and installer.

CONSTRUCTION OF A SOLAR ENERGY SYSTEM

How can I make a rate-effective solar system?

The fight for electricity efficiency has in no way been waged with greater ultra-contemporary guns, and the winners are all folks who pay less for month after month.

A low-price solar panel tool could be the excellent answer for excessive strength payments.

Every yr solar panels become extra less expensive.

Solar panels are one shape of power tool.

They may be configured in homes regardless of an offline community.

Usually with grid-related structures solar electricity is used by many human beings an awesome way to hold coins in application payments.

To get the most out of sun strength at the same time as installing a miles much less high priced device , it's far encouraged to use appliances with the lowest energy rating .

If you have to now not have enough money to install a bigger machine try and keep away from big strength clients:

For example, immediately showers;

domestic heating;

air conditioners and so forth...

The layout of the complete device is the performance detail.

Each device is probably precise relying on the power requirements that the device desires to fulfill.

Even for a small sun device , there are various variables to keep in mind.

Compromises need to be made in a small, low-fee solar tool.

Designing your private sun gadget to harness sun electricity is a large venture, however it is able to be a amusing task for masses do-it-yourselfers or all people with engineering experience.

It is probably important to do some research and punctiliously plan the whole tool without forgetting to discover all important gadgets and collect allows.

It is more suitable to construct a small panel of a task, which encompass an RV backup electricity supply.

How to construct a solar panel tool?

Before looking for your device, bear in thoughts that sun cells on Internet sites are typically of decrease best...

They can be chipped, faulty or otherwise damaged, this is unwanted.

Here is a list of what is needed to bring together a sun panel device:

Configure and size your solar gadget constant collectively together with your energy wishes.

You will need to recognize how lots electricity you expect to apply on common according to month, further to how a good deal solar exposure you can expect at a few stage within the three hundred and sixty five days, to decide how many sun panels you may want.

Once you have got were given determined this, you can determine which emblem and model of sun panel fits you extremely good.

You will want fewer panels if you are coating a small mission or a lamp.

Simply calculate what number of kWh the device may additionally have, then multiply that range via manner of the amount of panels to be built.

Get the components of a solar panel this way.

You will want photovoltaic cells , pre-welded wiring, nonconductive material, and plexiglass.

The conversion of solar strength into energy is honestly counting on sun cells; each of the panels has a median of 36 cells inner it.

Buying a pre-soldered tab cord will save you some steps, but you may although need to have a soldering iron to do the wiring in the back of the cells and to run the twine connecting them.

Wood is normally used as a help fabric for DIY sun panels because it is simple to drill holes for wiring.

Once the sun cells are linked together, glue them to the timber help earlier than connecting them all and soldering each of the solar cells collectively.

After wiring, the ones wires are connected to a load, which adjusts the power volts.

Wood also may be used to bring together a field to defend the solar cells, that can then be protected with plexiglass for moisture safety.

After wiring and gluing the solar cells onto a wooden substrate, it is going to be important to seal them with to defend them from warmness, debris and moisture.

Suppose you are unsure of your potential to build sun panels from scratch.

If that is the case , you should purchase a sun panel package deal, that allows you to consist of extra commands unique to your panels.

Purchasing a sun package can be extra remarkable because it already includes cabinets.

The racking is tough;

it's far important to decide which shelving system is suitable for the particular type of floor meeting.

When you check the Web internet sites of vendors, you can find out that there's nearly an overabundance of mounting and meeting device to be had.

INSTALL YOUR OWN SOLAR PANEL RACK

Which opportunity to pick out on the time of purchase is determined via the usage of in which the panels is probably installed.

For example, will they be set up at the floor or in each other location?

This will decide the form of cabinets wanted.

As rapid as you have got had been given decided on your shelf, pick out in which to drill the holes so you can attach it to the form.

CONNECT SOLAR PANELS TO SHELVES

You will want suitable clamps or connectors for determined on racks to attach solar panels to gadget.

Buying them collectively and from the equal distributor guarantees that they're designed for every special.

Solar panel kits normally encompass racks, in case you buy the whole thing separately make sure you have were given a totally functioning electricity tool.

INSTALL THE APPROPRIATE SOLAR INVERTER

Installing a solar inverter requires technical data as it want to be related to the strength grid.

It is strongly endorsed to rent a expert to do this, as he or she can do it virtually and correctly with the important permissions.

Specifications whilst developing your very very personal tool

Solar panels which can be commercially produced come at a higher fee.

Solar cells are broadly to be had international and may be coupled with custom designed solar panels.

You can also discover broken cells however although in the marketplace;

those will despite the fact that art work and permit you to create one almost for not something.

As you assemble your panel take into account to be aware about this stuff:

CELL VOLTAGE AND POWER

Creating your personal sun panel is tremendous in that you may gather it in step with your dreams.

Solar cells commonly are to be had 0.Five V and a number of watt outputs,

you can join them in sere and produce any output voltage (in multiples of zero.5V).

If you want to rate a discharged 12V battery for an off-grid software program application, you may need an 18V battery together with 36 cells related in series.

18 V is required absolutely so the panel can price the battery even supposing it is not exposed to daylight.

You can strive dividing the sun cells through a better voltage of each cellular based at the range of cells needed.

Then you may furthermore have to recall the quantity of electricity.

Divide the entire electricity required through the cellular power to decide the amount of solar cells favored.

For instance, in case you need a panel of and you are the usage of 4 W cells, you need 2 hundred W / 4 W = 50 cells.

It should be cited that whether or not or no longer they may be related in collection or parallel does not have an effect on the strength.

Chapter 4: Arrangement Of Solar Panels

You need to start thru making plans the panel format.

This is typically executed relying on the amount available for the panel;

you is probably confined with the useful resource of the duration or width of the panel, but you can modify the alternative factors to fit your desires.

A 0.Five x 6 m sheet of glass become used for the 9 sun cells and that they have been prepared as confirmed inside the linked diagram.

It doesn't rely how many rows and columns there are inside the panel, but it permits lots if you create longer strings of cells within the direction of the tabulation, and then combine them with the thread along the top and backside.

SOLAR PANEL TABLE

Cataloging solar cells is the subsequent and longest step.

You should purchase pre-cut cells in case you are not acquainted with using a soldering iron, but most sun cell suppliers will provide you with those without a desk.

Once you have got mastered the method, it isn't tough, but you could need to exercise on one or first because the board is difficult to remove.

For the terminal forums, you want to reduce the cord a hint longer than the length of 1 cellular, times the duration of each cell for the boards.

Immediately begin soldering the wire from the board to the sun mobile.

To begin, use the glide pen to attract a line along the silver traces.

Then skip the recent soldering iron over the entire tab after coating the tab cord at the tab lines themselves.

If the soldering iron is left in place for too lengthy, it'll overheat and harm the mobile.

Since the board cable is gift, no soldering needs to be brought.

BUS CABLE CONNECTION

Once you have got were given classified all of your cells, you could need to connect them.

The the front of each cellular is terrible, on the same time as the lower back is first rate.

These should be related in collection like batteries forming a the front cell chain.

You need to ultimately solder the wires from the decrease lower back tab of 1 to the the the front of the following mobile till the street is entire.

The bus cable is then used to connect the traces.

The final layout need to resemble the sample to begin with created.

When connecting the lines, be aware that they've to be related awesome to terrible in order that the lines run in opposite recommendations.

When you have got have been given finished connecting your traces, you could have a high best bus and a horrific bus, which outputs your sun panels.

These can be soldered at once onto the wires or into a very precise solar panel housing for the panels.

PROTECT CELLS WITH GLASS

Once the bus cables are completed, solar cells with protective glass or plexiglass may be used.

Apply a non-prevent bead of silicone throughout the fringe panel of the holder, then gently slide the glass from the cells.

The silicone have to form a non-save you seal for the duration of the panel, defensive the cells.

Let the silicone dry in a unmarried day via manner of locking the glass and returned panel collectively.

Instead of screw clamps, which provide an excessive amount of clamping stress and can wreck the glass, use plastic spring clamps.

COMPARISON OF SOLAR CHARGE CONTROLLERS

What is a photovoltaic price controller?

The price controller regulates the amount of contemporary attaining the battery from the PV panels, starting the go together with the waft to the battery as speedy as it's far charged.

CRITERIA FOR CHOOSING THE CHARGE CONTROLLER

Two tremendous guidelines exercising:

1) Maximum modern output from the panels -> pick out a load controller that permits a barely higher present day.

2)For voltage, there should now not be many because of the reality all current regulators help voltages that mechanically 12 and 24 V.

Here are the overall recommendations for choosing the proper rate controller between MPPT and PWM with admire for your PV:

• MPPT fee controller

• Panel 36 from cells with 12V batteries

• forty eight-mobile panel with 12/24V batteries

• fifty four-cellular panels with a few 12/24V batteries

• seventy -cell panels with a few 12/24V batteries

• one hundred forty 4-cell panels with 48V batteries

CHOICE OF CHARGE CONTROLLER: ENVIRONMENTAL CONDITIONS AND ELECTRICAL PERFORMANCE

Here are some of the competencies to preserve in thoughts at the same time as choosing a fee controller.

First of all, the environmental working situations should be taken below attention: if the controller's installation situations are especially intense, the sort of the declared walking temperatures need to be taken into account.

The electrical customary overall performance have to be considered , so have a look at the voltage window of the PV generator with the coupling window in order that they may be correct;

confirm that the most generator input modern and maximum load functionality are not immoderate for the tool, and check the self-intake underneath one-of-a-type running situations.

CHOOSING A CONTROLLER TAILORED TO THE PLANT

The foremost skills of a rate controller , said in its specs, are:

the sun modern-day, this is the most current from the photovoltaic panels, identical to the sum of the rating cutting-edge-day of the photovoltaic panels even as related in parallel with each exceptional;

the nominal load contemporary , that is primarily based upon at the most of the AC-powered gadgets and the pinnacle;

The machine voltage, which may be 12V or 48V.

MAINTAINING A LOAD

A photovoltaic charge controller calls for no preservation apart from periodic tests of the cables that hook up with one of a type components of the device to make certain that they may be sealed and free of corrosion.

In addition, if the fee controller had been to be damaged, the financial results for the customer is probably great, as they'll moreover ought to replace the batteries.

A price controller need to be set up out of direct sunlight and in an area with exceptional airflow : in fact, even though modern-day rate controllers are robotically very strong, performance and sturdiness are affected by excessive warm temperature.

As a similarly protection mechanism to keep the charge controller, batteries, and gadgets and to reduce the risk of hearth, a fuse of suitable rating ought to be positioned between them and the rate controller itself.

HOW TO PERFORM PROPER MAINTENANCE OF THE SOLAR POWER SYSTEM AND BATTERIES

Maintenance of photovoltaic structures is crucial to ensure inexperienced sun energy: panels which is probably commonly clean and functioning make certain immoderate productivity and first-rate economic economic financial savings on software program bills.

The GSE has moreover currently expressed its perspectives on this problem, publishing a report containing strategies for managing the upkeep and technological modernization of incentivized plants.

Maintenance of panels, inverters, batteries, and PV device additives is regularly left out, each by means of way of owners and installers themselves.

The latter, even, very regularly do not even embody the services covered in on line PV charges.

Maintenance can be very vital and have to be finished every year, earlier than the summer time period, to make certain that the whole lot is on foot properly and that, as an example, in some unspecified time in the future of the season, low temperatures and snow masses have not affected the operation of the panels.

Those who have a photovoltaic tool with Energia incentives, this is, mounted earlier than July 2013, often have more troubles than others, due to the fact the employer that has inverters and panels for them may also moreover additionally now not exist and may not carry out routine and tremendous maintenance.

To solve this insidiousness, it is possible to show to stable and licensed groups that take care not high-quality of installations, however moreover of all cleansing and photovoltaic structures.

Just to frame the hints for plant upkeep , the GSE has drafted the record " Operation of Photovoltaic Plants, Maintenance Interventions and Technology Modernization" that mean guidelines for growing the strength and shipping of the photovoltaic device.

What does protection of a photovoltaic tool encompass?

The file launched via the GSE reads as:

Maintenance manner all ordinary and notable technical sports sports geared toward maintaining or restoring the capability and performance of a device, wherein: capability way the functionality to offer the overall performance expected inside the manufacturing format, general performance method the purpose and capability to offer the above offerings below applicable situations in phrases of economic gadget, operation, protection and environmental friendliness.

What interventions are wanted in element?

You also can perform simplest a number one check.

Visual inspection via the device owner is a smooth and smooth approach, if to be had.

By looking on the panels, you may have a study viable breaks and brief contact technical agency.

To keep away from drops in overall performance and save you system malfunction, that may jeopardize state incentives from the GSE, it's miles first-class to use corporations that specialize in maintenance structures.

Here are the interventions that can be requested and recommended by using sun professionals.

Panel washing : to be accomplished at least as quickly as a 365 days, via corporations ready with machines capable of removing scale and impurities.

Biennial photovoltaic device record: maintainers conduct tests to certify the operation of devices and confirm the scenario of modules.

Instrumental exams: simulation of plant operation to affirm its normal usual performance underneath actual weather situations.

Check GSE place of job paintings to make certain you get incentives and presents for on-net site trade.

PHOTOVOLTAIC STORAGE: BATTERY MAINTENANCE

Many families have determined on to combine an electricity garage tool into their PV device.

They have finished so due to the reality they're aware about the gain that power storage can offer, as well as the first rate impact that this sort of sustainable choice has at the environment.

Of direction, considering that that is an digital machine , it too desires periodic tests.

An annual check of the garage system is normally recommended, with verification of battery integrity and right inverter operation.

Although accumulators require little or no renovation , to ensure that the whole lot is so as , we propose activating a 24/7 monitoring provider.

In this manner, you are constantly associated with the center, which is ready to intervene if productiveness is interrupted.

And with the app you can: test the quantity of managed products, consumption, command the switching on and off of circle of relatives domestic machine to apply at once from the app and in actual time, the overall performance of the panels even in case you are not at home.

Now allow's take a look at the safety of photovoltaic batteries.

Batteries also are a key detail in ensuring that your system is at its maximum green.

Of path, because of the reality that storage systems are always gadgets, they will additionally need periodic tests.

In this regard, it is endorsed which you conduct a take a look at-up of your storage device, which encompass a check of the batteries and the right functioning of the inverter.

In addition, one element to be considered to save you any issues related to the safety of garage systems concerns their installation.

A battery is generally installation close to the inverter;

there are, however, types of storage structures that can be absolutely incorporated, and their state-of-the-art layout moreover permits them to be set up as "furniture" internal your property.

In large, it's miles critical that the battery be composed of cells and located in a location big enough to make certain correct air go with the float.

Although storage systems require little safety, to make certain the whole thing is working properly, we endorse a regular monitoring provider with considered one in every of many apps, 24 hours an afternoon, seven days each week.

With an app you will be constantly associated with the operations middle and may:

• Check the quantity of energy produced

• Check consumption

• Monitor the battery output and abnormalities present.

In this context, it's far consequently vital which you carry out meticulous and periodic safety of your dell and your PV batteries!

WAYS TO PREVENT SHORT CIRCUITS AND FIRE HAZARDS SOLAR PANEL INSTALLATION

PV structures on hearth: right here's why!

When faced with a fireplace in a PV machine, it's miles first critical to recognize whether or not the begin of the fireplace is outdoor or inner to the gadget.

The maximum not unusual causes of fires in vegetation are:

Slow wiring and connectors, tightening screws.

If unfastened screw connections are detected, those need to generate an electrical arc that could cause fireside.

The electric powered arc generated on the identical time because the gadget is in operation ignites the underlying fabric, that is slowly fueled until the fireside develops.

A DC arc, at the voltage utilized in photovoltaic structures, can stay lit for only a few mins.

Therefore, it is probably to puncture a galvanized sheet than is usually used to help the panels on the roof and might reason ignition of the underlying substances.

It is also feasible for an arc to increase inside the panel because of defects at the intermediate aspect many of the cell and the cell or through oxidation because of a leakage of the panel seal.

The sluggish connections of the framework and the unique place of the give up of the slope can create seepage that through the years can generate, inside the route of immoderate quick-circuit currents, a fire;

Phenomenon called hot spot, or localized heating.

In modules, it's far not possible for all PVs to be perfectly identical due to the inevitable slight in production.

It also can show up that part of the FTV is shaded or maybe genuinely dirtier, strings of modules connected in parallel will in no way have the same voltage.

As a give up end result, an internal opposite present day must rise up, that might cause localized damage or overheating of the latest spot.

To avoid this, special diodes are inserted into the electric circuits whose lacking, or missing features are placed correctly, and the fabric used is checked for suitability,

Neglecting those factors can reason heat advantage that may motive risky outcomes;

Another of the weaknesses of the FTV gadget are the cables, which, with the shortage of insulation, can create arcing along the sections amongst string panels and/or inverters.

In specific, the cables need to be immune to radiation and immoderate temperatures, have an specific sufficient flow segment, and be properly related;

INVERTER OVERHEATING

Because the inverter is generally located in a totally particular housing, ignition also can unfold effortlessly.

When a PV plant is laid low with fireside, it is crucial to right now strong the regions which have been affected so that you can lessen/limit feasible soil-air contamination, to disconnect all affected elements from the power grid then proceed to the nation manufacturing facility vicinity.

Sanitization sports encompass the right disposal of the elements that were laid low with the fireplace: modules, cables, panels, and so on... (classifiable as mainly risky cloth) the following step is the sanitization and cleansing of the elements laid low with the fireside with any metal components that have been maximum affected, due to the reality the combustion of the PVC contained in the cable insulation releases, in the gaseous section, chlorine, which binds to shape hydrochloric acid, which may be very corrosive.

In case of a hearth growing in soil systems, analysis of the water table and close by aquifers want to be accomplished so one can rule out soil, subsoil or water contamination.

Speaking of prevention, it's miles proper to consider the following strategies:

Periodic exams on tightening of cables and wiring;

Checking cable insulation to prevent current leakage and short circuits;

Thermography on PV modules and the whole electric powered device to come to be aware of faults or warmth phenomena;

Module cleansing useful to avoid overheating of cells because of the development of feasible reverse currents;

EVERYTHING YOU NEED TO KNOW ABOUT SOLAR ENERGY

Solar power is the maximum essential renewable electricity deliver on the planet, and hundreds of strategies to take benefit of it were explored.

Given its considerable significance, the query arises: what are the traits of sun strength?

It is inexhaustible, it is on hand to all, and most significantly, it's miles smooth;

In fact, it involves no emission of CO_2 or particulate rely.

Having mentioned the appropriate features and importance of it, it's far viable at this point to offer an cause of the way the electricity is used and in what context;

this electricity supply is used for electricity and heat production by using sun radiation.

In cutting-edge years, the technological improvement of solar and photovoltaic structures has reached large tiers;

now that situation for the surroundings has end up increasingly more crucial, in towns and towns in extremely-current we're able to see more and more roofs with photovoltaic or sun panels.

How sun energy works

To better apprehend the capability of this inexperienced useful useful resource, it's far beneficial to recognize how solar energy is harnessed, what capability it has, and what its drawbacks are.

First, it's miles thrilling to understand that sun strength is an inexhaustible energy supply; the amount of radiant energy wearing out the Earth from the Sun steady with unit place is 1.Four kW/m².

As stated earlier, it's miles viable to advantage thermal energy from solar energy;

What are the precept techniques of appearing those skills?

• Solar photovoltaic: the precept problem of the gadget are photovoltaic panels, which encompass a series of cells able to reworking solar radiation into energy due to the presence of a semiconductor cloth, especially silicon.

Semiconductor substances, whilst touched via daytime, have the ability to generate a go together with the go with the flow of strength through the motion of electrons.

● Solar thermal: solar radiation additionally can be used to warmness domestic water or rooms , every in houses and organizations.

The number one tool of the solar thermal device is exactly the thermal one: its cause is to warmth a liquid warmth switch fluid, which then movements indoors bringing heat to the popular areas.

● Solar thermodynamic: a sun thermodynamic system is a generation that integrates a heat pump into the thermal machine.

What distinguishes it from awesome systems that use renewable power is the truth that this device operates yr-spherical and all day extended because of the presence of the warm temperature pump on which the unavailable sun power intervenes: the present day era this is used permits the system to feature unconditionally , without being restricted whilst the weather isn't the first-rate.

Advantages and disadvantages of sun electricity

Solar electricity, as we've got already stated, has blessings, each environmentally and economically.

In truth, the Sun is a inexperienced strength supply, associated with no gasoline combustion and no carbon emission.

It furthermore offers no problems: the complete Earth is irradiated through the Sun, no matter the fact that certainly a few regions are greater uncovered.

From an monetary element of view, the blessings are large: if, as an example, the installation of a photovoltaic device is big sufficient, the investment stays amortized over years: to offer a concrete instance, the whole A three kW set up calls for a reasonably sizeable price, recoverable interior an average of 8 years way to monetary financial savings on the bill and deductions that inspire the use of those modes of power supply.

In addition to this, in case you choose out the selection of PV with garage, you can achieve power bill savings of 90%.

However, solar strength moreover has terrible factors : one in each of them is that, solar irradiation is not non-stop due to alternating sunlight hours and weather activities at night, and quinei continuity of producing is not assured .

To triumph over this hassle, you may choose a photovoltaic device with garage, to have electricity although the device does not produce any.

The sun thermal tool, alternatively, already consists of the installation of the garage tank.

Chapter 5: How To Use Solar Energy

The splendid opportunity for harnessing solar energy is photovoltaics, a device that can transform sun radiation into electricity.

This machine may be used every in an environment through residential photovoltaics , in addition to in agency and employer settings but moreover for large-scale strength era.

To hold the electricity made from every day with the goal of distributing it higher pendant the opportunity periods, storage of the proper duration can be hooked up.

Green power additionally can be used to strength systems which incorporates radiant panel heating, or warm temperature pump for sustainable cooling and heating of homes.

Another way to warmth sun electricity is with a solar thermal, a device with precise solar panels that may use sun electricity right away for domestic warmness water manufacturing.

Solar thermal is also a very environmentally excellent solution with 0 emissions, plus solar thermal is collectively with large-scale systems, suitable for the strength wishes of hospitality centers, hospitals and condominium houses.

The concord of layout, installation of systems using sun, which embody photovoltaic and solar thermal , with right information of the energy that may definitely come from the solar makes it easy to installation this new strength.

Considering perfect conditions, for a solar panel, that is, located perpendicular to the solar's rays and interference from the Earth's surroundings, the radiant strength constant with meter on Earth is 1,366.Nine W/squarem.

This approach that every square meter of sun module achieves 1,366.Nine sun watts.

Radiant power is also known as irradiance, a unit of size that varies relying on the gap from the Earth to the Sun, the Earth's surroundings and the meteorological situations of the Sun's unique characteristic at a few stage in the day.

These elements make the floor illuminance certainly one of a kind in each place, in truth in keeping with ENEA in Italy solar radiation varies from a hundred and sixty W/m² inside the Po Valley to two hundred W/m² in Sicily.

Of direction, there are precise gadgets to degree sun radiation, inclusive of the pyranometer and pyroheliometer.

The thermal energy generated by way of the use of solar radiation is measured in watts or joules.

The strength produced via a photovoltaic machine is measured in kilowatts regular with hour to recognise the amount produced every 60 minutes.

How solar electricity is received

Energy from the Sun is received thru sun thermal panels, thru which sun radiation may be transformed into electric or thermal energy.

In photovoltaic structures, silicon cells are with the resource of sun irradiation, with electricity switch from moderate to electrons within the photovoltaic panel material.

This approach generates direct electric powered modern-day-day, it truly is transformed with the aid of the PV inverter to alternating modern-day-day in order that it is able to be used for self-intake or switch to electricity.

In PV systems with storage, unconsumed power is stored in unique batteries, so it is able to furthermore be used later, optimizing the overall performance of the system and the charge of self-intake.

A solar thermal gadget makes use of the solar's rays to transform solar energy into thermal electricity, thanks to special solar gadgets with which the convector heater is heated and the fluid with which the water is heated for heat exchange.

In this way it is also feasible to have water for sanitary capabilities without generating CO_2 emissions, and heating houses in an environmentally first-rate and sustainable way , way to 'solar electricity.

HOW TO CHOOSE YOUR SOLAR SYSTEM COMPONENTS SEPARATELY AND ASSEMBLE THEM INDEPENDENTLY TO REDUCE INSTALLATION COSTS

How do accumulators artwork?

This is a fairly contemporary era; until a few years ago, extra electricity can also moreover want to pleasant be recovered by using using on-net internet web page change, that is, via injecting the percentage no longer inside the strength grid.

Currently, but, manner to this energy garage gadget, it can be saved and ate up when wished.

Thus, domestic garage structures allow for improved self-intake, decreased off-top grid withdrawal, and additional economic savings on software payments.

Also, you may installation them without dropping the ones you used for sun panels.

Accumulators vs UPS

These accumulators ought to not be pressured with uninterruptible energy materials or UPS, which preserve electric and photovoltaic devices constantly powered.

They are continuously photovoltaic batteries that don't activate in an emergency, to keep away from electricity failure with the resource of manner of creating sure energy.

If a famous storage gadget is favored, only people with CEI 0-21 certification have to be installed at the strength grid.

According to the suggestions, an accumulator is defined because the set of gadgets, device and control and control accurate judgment, purposeful for the absorption and healing of electrical electricity.

Operates constantly, in parallel with the grid with a connection obligation and the possibility of associated with an change operation with the energy grid

In precis, UPS structures can not be like accumulators due to the fact they're meant first-rate for emergencies and are not designed to perform continuously.

Which one to select out?

There are three strategies to put in storage structures: the batteries and the tool are located most of the panels and the inverter, on the strength issue;

Post-manufacturing: batteries are positioned after the counter.

These are kits introduced to the tool with out changing the operation of the inverter;

Two-manner positioned up-manufacturing: batteries also can be charged with traditional energy.

Most structures can most effective be powered with the useful useful resource of photovoltaic panels and are consequently unidirectional.

On-grid and off-grid systems

Despite this, storage can notwithstanding the reality that supply power to the grid.

The systems can, in truth, be networked, then powered thru a separate package , along with a manipulate gadget and covered batteries or impartial.

Off-grid systems, but, are called structures due to the reality they do no longer feed the strength produced into the grid; they may best visit batteries.

Once loaded, manufacturing stops.

What characteristics to assess?

To pick out the proper type of garage, one should first keep in thoughts the dimensions and kind of PV batteries.

They will want to be sized correctly consistent with the strength you want.

Calculate that the not unusual power call for of a family is set 3000 kWh/twelve months, so about eight.2 kWh/day, and thinking about that intake takes place at night time, batteries provide approximately 4 kWh in line with day to significantly reduce your strength.

The advantages of the submitting tool

From an economic aspect of view, combining a gadget with an gift PV machine permits the initial one to be profitable in a suitable time , great 6 years if the device is 5 kWh and 10 years for greater than 5kWh.

This increases the output of the PV machine through approach of 50 to 80% in most notable instances.

The percentage finished relies upon on the scale of the system, your consumption, and the batteries you select out.

The use of electricity garage remains mainly more youthful, however if the product is well sized and combined with a clever control device, it can generate financial economic financial savings over the years, even with out incentives.

EVERYTHING YOU NEED TO KNOW ABOUT BATTERIES, SOLAR PANELS, INVERTERS, CHARGE CONTROLLERS, GENERATORS, CABLES, DEVICES, AND MANY OTHER THINGS

Photovoltaic accumulators: the principle types

Choosing the superb storage batteries for a machine manner finding the right trade-off among performance, durability, and client investment.

The gain of a garage system is that it could acquire products from sun radiation for use even within the midnight or nighttime hours- that is why the tool need to be designed all of the way right down to the smallest element in order that it can characteristic at its high-quality.

Accumulators are truly a key detail in undertaking high-quality normal basic performance, however what are the options in the marketplace?

Here are the principle sorts.

1. Lead-acid and lithium batteries.

The maximum famous kinds of accumulators are in reality lead-acid and lithium batteries.

Lead-acid batteries are the great solution for individuals who want to combine super widespread usual overall performance with funding expenses, no matter the reality that they have got the downside of being cumbersome and on commonplace heavier than the others.

They ought to additionally be located in nicely-located regions to prevent the discharge of hydrogen, mixed with oxygen, from producing explosive gases.

Of this kind, open and airtight accumulators are awesome: within the former case, water evaporates by using manner of electrolysis; in the latter, hydrogen recombines with oxygen and therefore, creates water all yet again.

Airtight accumulators encompass batteries: they do now not contain liquid acid but a pitcher microfiber absorbent;

Gel batteries: the electrolyte is absorbed.

2. Lithium batteries

Equally popular are lithium batteries, or lead-acid generation batteries.

Contrary to what has been seen before, lithium-ion batteries can discharge to greater than eighty%,

Have an average existence span this is twice as long;

• Are more regular;

• recharge in much less time.

It is obvious, however, that within the face of superior generation, not only does the general overall performance of these kinds of accumulators increase however additionally the value required for the investment.

three. Nickel-cadmium batteries

Nickel-cadmium batteries have a comparable form to guide-acid batteries, except that they use nickel hydroxide for the anode plates and nickel oxide for the cathode.

What characterizes NiCd batteries is their ordinary overall performance even at low temperatures-a detail to bear in mind if the PV machine is to be set up in specially cold regions.

Another gain is that the ones batteries can be discharged, on the equal time as in terms of general performance they continue to be on the extent of lithium batteries.

The dangers?

• better expenses than lithium;

• It has a tendency to discharge faster;

• hassle in disposing of cadmium, a specifically toxic material.

Nickel-metal-hydride batteries are a modern-day-day evolution of batteries: they provide better trendy overall performance and reduced impact, however moreover they have got better costs.

4. Salt batteries

While lithium batteries are the maximum wellknown in the PV marketplace, the look for however green and environmentally sustainable era has sincerely now not stopped.

Salt batteries, as an example, can be those that allows you to need to take delivery of precise hobby within the coming years: irrespective of the fact that also within the experimental and finding out phase, the modern-day studies are showing comforting outcomes in terms of each performance and energy economic savings.

In addition, sodium batteries want to take away combustion and threatening emissions , toward increasingly "inexperienced" and environmentally pleasant structures.

The global of Solar Panels: the entirety you want to apprehend

Photovoltaic panels: an define

If you are drawing near the area of sun panels for the first time, it is regular to invite your self a few questions about what they may be, how they paintings, how loads, and most significantly whether or not or no longer it is able to virtually save you cash in your software payments and shield the environment.

Throughout this summary, we're capable of answer your questions.

What are they?

A photovoltaic panel is a planar form composed of one of the photovoltaic cells associated in parallel and in series.

These cells are covered with a protecting glass whose purpose is to optimize the panel's general usual performance, on the same time as on the outside the rims are aluminum to growth the panel's solidity

How do they artwork?

The operation of a photovoltaic panel consists of the subsequent steps:

Expose the panel to the solar

Energy switch from photons to electrons on the silicon cellular;

CREATION OF ELECTRICITY IN THE CIRCUIT

Photovoltaic panels generate direct cutting-edge, they can not be used internal our housing!

This type of contemporary ought to then be converted to alternating contemporary via the use of a photovoltaic inverter , in order that it may then be used in the home.

Tilt and orientation

The excellent orientation of PV modules is toward the south.

However, it's far vital to keep in mind factors:

The orientation and slope of the roof of the house.

In Italy, on not unusual, the great tilt of photovoltaic panels is among 30° and 40°.

In this regard, it's far proper to bear in mind that the roof of the residence is flat, there are unique structures for photovoltaic panels that allow the roof to tilt and ensure most standard overall performance.

All outdoor marketers that would have an effect on the ground of the panels.

Shadows are also each special essential issue of putting in a sun system, as they have got an effect at the highest exceptional operation of the panel.

One feasible method to the effects of shading can be determined in the installation of optimizers, gadgets that allow the machine to characteristic nicely, although it's a ways a shaded panel.

PRICES

The costs of photovoltaic panels depend greatly on their energy and type.

There are 3 varieties of solar panels :

Monocrystalline silicon sun panels

Polycrystalline silicon photovoltaic panels

Thin-movie solar panels

2020 have grow to be an uncommon yr for absolutely everyone, and 2021 seems to be the twelve months of financial recuperation.

This circumstance, delivered to the advertising and marketing of renewable strength, has advanced global name for for sun panels through 10 percentage.

With the increase in name for came the problem of shortage of materials and the ensuing growth in costs.

THE BENEFITS

There are many hidden benefits behind putting in a panel:

Energy monetary monetary savings: installing photovoltaic panels may be an luxurious investment within the starting, however the economic savings finished on the fee are visible from the primary bill.

In addition, the extra energy produced can be fed into the grid and "provided."

On common in Italy, putting in the proper gadget saves between 60% and 70% of electricity costs, getting higher the funding in lots much less than 5 years.

Sustainability: in contrast to distinct property of electricity , panels will let you generate smooth strength at km0 on the equal time as retaining the environment.

Availability: the solar is an inexhaustible supply of strength, that is why it can be generated even inside the most far off regions of the planet.

Insurance and guarantee on photovoltaic panels

To amazing shield your solar panels , you need to understand what types of coverage exist and which ones is the extraordinary.

Photovoltaic structures are not the best ones that want a insurance.

Solar systems want to additionally be insured.

What sorts of sun panels exist?

In what troubles the kinds of photovoltaic panels, it is good to differentiate modules that are used for power from those which can be used to warmth water.

Therefore, the primary sorts of solar modules are:

Photovoltaic sun panels

SOLAR THERMAL PANELS

Solar photovoltaic panels can be divided in a single-of-a-type techniques, which incorporates:

• Their use

• The material they will be made of

• The peak electricity

• The dimensions

• Types of solar panels consistent with their use

• Depending on the use of photovoltaic panels, the ones may be:

• For residential use

• For business use

• Used in sun farms in which solar electricity is on a huge scale

TYPES OF SOLAR PANELS ACCORDING TO THEIR MATERIAL

PV modules also may be divided thru kind and operation.

In this situation we distinguish:

• Monocrystalline silicon panels

- Polycrystalline silicon panels

- Amorphous silicone panels

In addition, the factors and materials that make up a PV are:

- Base of help

- Ethylene Vinyl Acetat

- Photovoltaic cell

- Tempered glass

- Aluminum frame

- Injunction concern

Recall that the environmental effect of photovoltaic panels comes from the materials they will be made from.

Usually pleasant one form of panel is typically endorsed: monocrystalline photovoltaic modules , that have more capability than one-of-a-type kinds for solar strength generation.

Types of solar panels in keeping with their top electricity output:

When we speak approximately the electricity of a solar panel, we communicate with its capability to deliver photovoltaic electricity under top-rated situations.

This is expressed in pinnacle watts.

On this basis, residential PV modules usually have an output of about 375 Wp.

TYPES OF SOLAR PANELS ACCORDING TO THEIR SIZE

Given their duration, photovoltaic modules include:

Usually the type used for domestic photovoltaic systems is one which include 60 cells.

In phrases of duration, the 60 sun panels degree 164 cm x ninety nine cm, at the identical time because the seventy two-mobile PV measures approximately 2 mx m.

It is essential to mention, the various one-of-a-kind types of solar panels available on the market, solar modules.

This form of photovoltaic panel ensures every the production of energy to strength the home equipment in our homes and the manufacturing of water and heat air to heat our rooms.

Many economic financial savings can be accomplished through hybrid panels along with:

Increased strength production : hybrid panels offer a extraordinary gain, especially, they may be cooled.

In truth, way to the air flow of the air hybrid panels and the water exchanger of the water hybrid panels, the sun modules can be cooled to permit better performance at some level in the yr;

Savings on heating : Solar panels use their warm temperature to warm temperature your private home, consequently having a one-of-a-type impact for your heating bill;

Hot water economic savings: warm temperature produced through hybrid solar panels may be used to provide home warmth water.

If you study the charge of hybrid solar panels with the rate of photovoltaic panels, you will be aware that the preceding is drastically better.

In standard, the fee of a three kWp hybrid tool costs approximately €15,000, this is an lousy lot better than the charge of a 3 kWp PV device, this is spherical €6,000.

THE ENVIROMENTAL IMPACT OF PHOTOVOLTAIC PANELS

The introduction of a solar module is an extended complex way divided into numerous ranges:

- Silicon fabrication

- Electric circuit printing

- Connection of photovoltaic cells

This manufacturing manner requires a large amount of power, mainly within the glass and silicon melting degree.

And this is why a direction of virtually popular adoption of renewable energy has began in the area of hybrid photovoltaic panels as nicely.

In fact, we are able to see how solar panel approaches evolve from 365 days to 365 days becoming greater inexperienced and consuming a good deal less power.

In addition, it want to additionally be talked about that on the equal time as producing energy, sun panels do now not emit any environmentally harmful materials.

Their manufacturing, transportation and recycling have a low effect on the surroundings.

In addition, all through its lifetime , a panel produces an awful lot extra power than it requires for its manufacturing.

Therefore, its impact at the environment is amazing, and making an funding in a solar system is absolutely the awesome choice as it does unique for the planet.

Disposal of solar panels

Before dealing particularly with PV panel disposal techniques, it is ideal to understand the "WEE"

In fact, WEE stands for " waste device and electronics," and this elegance includes sun.

Obviously, the elimination of WEE and photovoltaics especially want to be completed in an environmentally exceptional dynamic.

Assuming that each one the substances that make up photovoltaics are considerably recyclable, as they may be composed in particular of aluminum, modules broken down into the special materials upon disposal comprehend low recycling.

• There are types of photovoltaic WEEs constant with their power output:

"professional": waste generated via the usage of photovoltaics installed in systems with a rated energy of extra than 10 kW.

• "Household": waste generated with the resource of solar panels set up in establishments with a rated output of less than 10 kW.

The disposal of a family plant want to be sorted via the owner at the applicable series center, which may be consequences determined from the reliable internet site of the coordinating center.

Since disposal is the responsibility of the manufacturer, the fee will no longer be borne through way of the proprietor and can be freed from rate.

In precis, "family" PV, having reached the surrender of its existence, ought to be sent with the useful resource of the Manager to a Collection Center , so one can resultseasily be able to tune it

consulting the institutional frame of the website online.

As said in advance, the fee of doing away with domestic PVs" in addition to the recuperation operations , are borne by way of the use of the producers, making the operation free of price for the solar device owner.

Slightly tremendous is the argument approximately the elimination of photovoltaic brought on strength invoice.

The incentive called the Energy Account consists of a financial contribution kWh of strength produced in a given length.

Currently the Conto Energia incentive is no longer applicable , the final one changed into in 2013.

Therefore, if you have supplied a sun tool using a government Conto Energia incentive, the GSE will preserve a part of the sum as a precautionary diploma of the ultimate 10 years proper to develop the future sale of sun panels .

As proof of proper disposal from the gadget, the panel may be again in one lump sum, 12 €/"circle of relatives" panel and 10 €/"expert" panel.

The man or woman in rate of "household" panels. , on the time of disposal, will pick whether or now not to take rate of the direct control of the panels, or at hand them over to a provider who will perform the waste disposal operations and their treatment.

However, beneath present day regulations, the producer-or owner-continues responsibility for the processing chain, notwithstanding the truth that the task is delegated to a third party.

INVERTERS:

An inverter is an digital device capable of remodeling modern-day from one united states to each exceptional, is an virtual device that ditransforms direct present day , from alternating contemporary at given voltage and frequency.

It is vital for powering, via contemporary, electric powered powered gadgets that deliver AC power.

In photovoltaic systems, its use is intuitive.

A photovoltaic machine produces direct present day, even as the house grid is powered by alternating cutting-edge.

The inverter, has precisely the venture of "reversing" the present day and transforming it into alternating contemporary-day.

Inverter, what is it for?

Let's say that we've got a device that runs on 230V alternating current but we do not have energy that offers us with alternating cutting-edge... Thanks to an inverter we're capable of power this tool with direct current in evaluation to that of a 12V battery produced through a device.

In electric powered cars, inverters redecorate the current saved in batteries.

PHOTOVOLTAIC INVERTER:

The inverter is a key element of a photovoltaic device.

As indicated it's far used to convert power produced as direct contemporary-day from photovoltaic panels, to 50Hz alternating current-day.

This conversion is vital in order that the strength produced by using using manner of the PV may be discharged into the general public grid to traditional 230V consumers.

In this case it's far a frequency inverter .

CONSTANT FREQUENCY INVERTER

Constant frequency inverters are also implemented in circle of relatives uninterruptible power resources or storage batteries.

In the UPS, the line voltage is continuously rectified to a degree like minded with the internal battery and is converted again to AC by means of manner of the inverter with desired at the identical time as energy outages get up.

There are uninterruptible strength components/accumulators with a big type of powers, from hundred-3 hundred watts or maybe extra than 30 kW.

Inverters for three-section cars, variable frequency drives

Frequency converters, however, are used to modify the rate of 3-phase motors: the rate of the motor is closely related to the frequency of the motor with which it's miles powered.

TYPES OF INVERTERS

There are numerous models of inverters, however the maximum popular are specially three in quantity and all capable of a sine or pseudo-sinusoidal wave.

Square wave inverter:

are extra suitable for in easy terms resistive loads.

MODIFIED SINE WAVE INVERTER:

dated for resistive or capacitive loads and plenty less appropriate for inductive masses due to the fact they're too noisy.

Pure sine wave inverter:

appropriate for all styles of masses due to the truth they have to faithfully reproduce a sine wave equal to what our domestic energy grid is.

Chapter 6: How An Inverter Works

Specifically, how does an inverter make alternating cutting-edge from direct present day-day?

To understand how an inverter works, you have to first apprehend how an alternator and transformer paintings.

By way of description simplest, the inverter can be considered a "modified" transformer with the addition of a transistor circuit.

inverter operation

The alternator is able to transforming mechanical electricity into electric powered electricity in the shape of alternating current-day-day via the phenomenon of electromagnetic induction, the maximum common being alternating bicycle ignitions on headlights or the hamster wheel, which at the same time as spinning are able to carry out a coil able to powering an electric powered bulb;

In truth, in its pleasant shape, the alternator is given by a coil of wire with a magnet.

When the magnet pole strategies the coil, brought on modern-day-day is created in the coil and could go together with the drift within the contrary path producing alternating modern-day.

Much more complicated is the operation of a transformer which, like the alternator, produces an induced alternating present day-day but this time in a variable magnetic discipline is via a further coil called the "number one coil" .

Operation of the coils

The coils are every passed through by using an alternating present day: if the path of the present day changes, the polarity of the magnetic problem changes.

In the transformer, the secondary coil can change the output produced through using the number one coil.

We need to visualize the coil as a spiral; if the coil will consist of double windings with recognize to the number one coil, the secondary coil can be capable of generate two times the voltage finished to the primary coil.

Thus, manner to the transformer, any version may be finished through converting the size of the coils.

If in the alternator the primary coil has direct modern-day-day flowing thru it, no delivered approximately modern-day might be shaped within the secondary coil due to the truth the magnetic field does no longer vary; if a non-save you and rapid alternate of path can be accomplished, then we've got direction reversal, which is finished by way of the use of manner of transistors or thyristors.

Here are some tips for calculating the intake and electricity of the satisfactory inverter and batteries to buy:

The tool for calculating how a fantastic deal our consumption is: A x V

To calculate the overall energy in Watt Hours, I want the previously calculated Watts from the expected time the power will remain on: Wh = W x T

To calculate the consumption in Ampere Hours that the software program program may also have almost approximately the battery, I want to divide by means of the Watt Hours: Ah= Wh / 10

The minimum capability of the battery must be at least two times the prevent stop end result obtained above.

133

To deliver a sensible example, allow's anticipate that our device runs for an hour and a 1/2 of, now permit's calculate the watts Now of consumption:

Wh= W x T Wh= 660W x 1.Five Wh= 990

We now calculate the intake in Ah to decide the capability of the corporation battery:

Ah= Wh / 10 Ah= 990 Wh / 10 Ah= ninety nine

This calculation tells us that to use my device, I will need an inverter of about 1000 W power and one or more batteries with a complete capability of hundred Ah.

HOW TO INSTALL AN INVERTER?

An inverter need to always be mounted close to the battery with cables no longer exceeding half of of a meter.

We need to locate a place to secure haven it; it ought to be dry and a long way from water.

The inverter need to be turned off in the zero function.

You want to then upload a fuse of suitable resistance to the crimson twine and join every wires to the inverter.

Connect the two cables to the battery, being cautious now not to opposite the polarity, and take a look at that the whole thing is tight.

How to use an inverter?

When we switch on the inverter, we want to attend at least seconds for it to heat up and be prepared.

We be part of the system we need to perform to the 220V outlet, and if the intake of the device exceeds the electricity of the inverter, it could sound a warning tone.

In the case of less expensive inverters , components may burn out because of overload.

Photovoltaic cells

Photovoltaic cells are the concept of sun structures that produce easy power.

These electric powered devices are capable of convert electricity into electricity thru exploiting the photovoltaic effect.

And the mobile is most effective a small but essential piece of the puzzle that makes up photovoltaic modules.

Now we will find out together how it's miles composed.

WHAT DOES A PHOTOVOLTAIC CELL LOOK LIKE?

Usually each cell is characterised by means of the use of a square form, the size of about 12.Five cm on a thing, and one which varies among 0.25 and 0.35 mm.

Silicon is the most well-known fabric for the ones solar cells.

However, the appearance of thin-movie structures has brought approximately the advent of latest compounds , which incorporates indium diselenide and cadmium telluride.

Photovoltaic electric devices have layers, bad and immoderate quality fee, respectively.

The photovoltaic cell, way to the photovoltaic effect, converts incident power into strength.

The form absorbs the photon, which enters with the extremely good layer of the cell.

As a end result of the adjacency with P, the photon is channeled to the circuit, because of this producing electricity.

The photovoltaic mobile represents simplest one of the solar cores.

Each cell is set up to the alternative with the useful resource of steel elements.

Their union gives upward push to the photovoltaic module, moreover referred to as the sun panel, the device that captures slight and initiates the technique of reworking energy.

The module is positioned on guide systems to permit for proper orientation and tilt.

ELECTRICAL CABLES

An electric powered cable is an electrical aspect which incorporates one in every of severa wires that act as electrical conductors, one spherical the alternative and guarded with one or more layers of fabric that act as electric powered insulation and safety.

Widely used within the vicinity of electrical engineering, telecommunications electronics, it has the characteristic of transmitting strength or replacing facts and information over a distance.

The set of pressured connections of a given community infrastructure or cable gadget , similarly to the interlacing and interlacing operation itself, is known as "cabling."

Almost all electrical cables use metals with low electric powered resistivity for the conducting wires.

These range in thickness relying on the modern-day-day load ability and whether or not or no longer or no longer immoderate mechanical stress resistance or better is sought;

They also may be twisted into spirals, flattened or shaped.

Cables are artifacts advanced essentially in period to attach factors that allows you to switch electric powered powered energy or information from one to a few different with the useful resource of electromagnetic fields.

In the former case we communicate of electrical cables, within the latter of telecommunication cables.

LAYING METHOD

Depending on the laying tool, cables commonly embody: overhead cables: those are laid on specific allows on wooden, steel or steel poles;

overland cables: the ones are buried immediately or in underground tunnels or particular tunnels at a depth of the ground to sufficiently protect them from moves that may be inadvertently finished on the ground;

submarine cables: rest on the lowest of the ocean, lakes or rivers of water, after possibly making a corridor freed from specific roughness in which the cable is probably trouble to precise constraints;

then you definately continue to cowl them with appropriate shielding layers.

There is also an intermediate category of cables known as manipulate and signaling cables, used to transmit electric electricity that is used to prompt the gadgets to which they may be linked.

Finally, at the same time as cables are undertaking to answers if you want to present them unique traits, as an instance thru operability even in especially aggressive environmental situations , they may be referred to as "unique cables."

Cables are stated to be "armored" if, similarly to the outside protection with which they're normally geared up, they will be in addition protected through the software program of aluminum lead pipes or strips/wires of spirally wound iron/steel and nicely dealt with for corrosion protection.

POWER CABLES

Energy cables encompass one or more factors known as cores.

Depending at the amount of nuclei , they're referred to as unipolar, bipolar, tripolar, quadrupolar, and masses of others.

and their huge variety is determined by means of manner of the electrical tool of which they'll be a thing.

Each center includes a conductor included through an insulator.

The skip phase of the conductor is based upon on the electric modern via which electric electricity is transmitted.

The large the conductor move-phase , the extra difficult it is to cope with the cable throughout its installation and use.

When it's miles important to decorate its flexibility, the conductor is instead of a single cord or a few large-segment wires strung collectively from many wires strung collectively.

The thinner the character strands, the greater possible the center can be.

For every phase and conductor length of a given cable, the producer units the bending radius underneath which it isn't important to transport whilst laying or the use of the cable so as no longer to compromise its integrity.

The insulation may be made from cloth fabric, paper, PVC-based totally totally compounds, polyethylene, or particular synthetic materials.

The thickness and technical trends of the insulation want to be that the particular conductors in no manner come into contact with each different and that, relying on the tendencies of the insulating material used, they're a protracted manner enough aside absolutely so the unique electric powered potentials gift amongst them do not deliver an electric surprise.

When the cores are not protected via manner of a material they're called naked cores.

The insulating fabric that maintains them aside is the air interposed amongst them, wherein case their installation should most effective be airborne.

Their allows want to be specifically insulated from the ground to disperse electrical electricity to the ground, and the gap among them and a few special surrounding devices want to be in all situations so as no longer to motive extremely dangerous electric powered powered shocks to human beings and belongings.

Electrical electricity is a feature of the product and contemporary-day flowing in conductors times the voltage existing the numerous conductors.

During transmission there are losses that depend essentially at the glide phase of the conductor.

These losses are expressed in warmth that increases the temperature of the conductors, for this reason weakening their mechanical resistance to strain and, beyond fantastic limits, compromising the dielectric houses of the insulator.

For each section of conductor, counting on the cloth the conductor itself and the insulator are made of, there is a modern fee that cannot be passed , every to restrict losses and because of the mechanical nonresistance of the center, that can impair the electric potential of the insulator.

To boom the strength and as a result the transmitted power, all that stays is to growth the voltage;

However, this calls for an boom in insulation and consequently inside the distance amongst conductors.

Beyond wonderful voltage values , the handiest feasible solution is overhead cables which include conductors and appropriate helps as a lot as the masts.

In this situation, the cable includes a difficult and rapid of 3 conductors which is probably part of an electrical machine.

Multiple triplets can be supported with the aid of manner of the identical set of trusses, from whose fingers an appropriate conductors are suspended.

To defend the conductors and the electrical tool of which it is part from hurricane discharges, a grounded conductor is laid over the conductors and supported with the useful

useful resource of the poles themselves, which acts as a lightning rod.

Conductors need to be capable of aid tensile stresses with the aid of manner of manner in their personal weight , for the section positioned among contiguous supports, with any greater weights and from the ones generated by using using wind.

Given the gap among sections, those are regularly excessive for a unmarried aluminum conductor,

In this example it need to be nicely strengthened.

The most often used method is to update any part of the conductive wires with comparable alloy wires that are stronger than the same aluminum and/or add steel wires which is probably greater evidence in the direction of tensile forces,

In the ones times we speak about strengthened conductor.

Underground cables must have insulated cores regardless of the truth that they may be part of the transmission network and are consequently excessive-voltage cables.

These cables have to have the equal voltage as the simplest they'll be part of.

The generation to offer the ones cables is state-of-the-art.

To save you floor discharges that arise at the ones voltages at the floor of the insulator, a layer of semiconductor material is located among the conductor and the insulator,

the identical is right most of the outer ground of the insulation and the overlapping layers.

This is finished with the beneficial useful resource of spiral strips of semiconductor paper or with the resource of using extrusion together with the insulation in an surroundings absolutely protected from pollutants or some different pollutant.

Equally today's and pricey is the technology for installing accent merchandise which includes insulators, fittings, terminals.

The use of those cables remains restricted.

When the transportation community crosses lake branches or basins or river basins and it isn't always possible to use strengthened overhead conductors , submerged power cables should be used.

Not extremely good the cables but additionally their management end up extremely-present day.

It is vital to use the more effective insulators than paper and fluid oil, which incorporates strips of the purest paper helically wound over the conductor and impregnated with treated and unique oils to get rid of any air bubbles and impurities, and/or to maintain the temperature of the conductors low through circulating coolants inner them at a managed temperature.

The distribution community consists in particular of cables with insulated rubber or flow-related polyethylene center, stranded covered by way of PVC sheathing buried in a built-up vicinity supported by means of using piling on the periphery.

In the latter case, the usage of cables with aluminum conductors insulated with skip-related polyethylene wrapped in an obvious spiral of metal cable assisting them is turning into increasingly more well-known;

on this way the stack can be an awful lot less dense, due to the fact the self-helping potential of the cable inside the section between contiguous ones is plenty more.

When there is a lot of electricity to transmit for an electrical, for instance due to the fact there are numerous low-consumption clients or few clients however high consumption, to limit losses it's far higher to transmit at intermediate voltage.

It will then be critical to have every different set of locations close to a smaller business company of consumer customers or without delay at the immoderate-consumption surrender character.

The network from the meter to the "electricity" of the mild factors or devices is known as the inner network and is owned through using the patron.

Power supply is single-phase low-voltage/biphase for offices and homes, three-phase for machines that deliver greater energy.

Indoor community cables are specifically assembled with PVC insulated conductors beneath PVC sheathing;

bendy conductors are used whilst laying requires smaller bending radii.

The cable sections from the sockets to the client's gadgets are pressured with conductors for easy dealing with.

In cases in which it is vital to have excessive resistance to warm temperature sources, which encompass connecting an iron , conductors are nearly continuously protected by using manner of material or silicone socks.

In a given territory, the transmission of power via clients takes location through a community of cables.

The element from the generators to the substations of neighboring utilities is known as the excessive- and medium-voltage transmission grid , the component from the transformers to the surrender customers is known as the distribution grid.

The interposition of transformer stations between the two grids is critical for strength to be transmitted in immoderate voltage in the transmission grid, in medium voltage or low voltage within the distribution grid, and the transition from one the voltage to the opposite takes vicinity precisely in transformer substations way to special transformers.

The immoderate-voltage transmission community consists mainly of bare-center cables supported with the resource of pylons.

Chapter 7: Why Does Sustainable Energy Matter?

In the sort of time we live in, there can be no question approximately the significance of manufacturing sustainable energy and retaining it. If the opportunity of absolutely switching to it exists (because it need to), even higher. However, not each person is familiar with its importance or why we need to.

Access to easy and secure energy it's also sustainable (renewable) has continuously been genuinely taken into consideration one among humanity's first-rate stressful conditions. The cutting-edge power supply we use is fossil fuels. This powers your homes, your cars and quite hundreds the whole lot else that requires power to transport. That's splendid, but it is also slowly destroying our surroundings. See, on every occasion you make use of fossil gasoline power, it emits carbon dioxide into our air. This reasons pollution, and the smog you notice setting like an ominous gray cloud above cityscapes.

You need it were no longer something but a cloud however the unhappy reality is that it isn't always and it truly contributes to hundreds of different problems as nicely. But earlier than we get to the consequences, allow's pass decrease lower returned to the very deliver. As mentioned in advance, one of the predominant reasons as to why there's too much carbon dioxide in our air, is the combustion (burning) of fossil fuels for strength. But to delve deeper can be complicated so allow's damage this down certainly thru looking at the top three carbon dioxide manufacturers and the manner we make a contribution to it.

1. Electricity

Fossil fuels electricity complete countries. So sincerely imagine how loads of it receives burned on a each day basis. Each time you open your tv or activate your fuel range to prepare a meal, you are the usage of it and producing carbon dioxide emissions. In truth, a single home can produce a whole of 12.Four masses of the stuff. That's lots specifically if you examine it on a grander scale. In reality, strength is the most important belongings of CO_2. But that is just from within the house, what approximately at the same time as we are outdoor?

2. Transportation

There's no actual give up near our carbon footprints. Whenever you pressure your car to paintings or to buy some issue from the grocery, you are burning up fossil fuel and generating carbon. This receives released immediately into our environment which it continuously bores a hole into. Transporting people and gadgets from one area to the opposite elements in at 32% with reference to the total $Co2$ emissions and that variety continuously grows as an increasing number of people pick out out to strain gasoline guzzling vehicles that produce large portions of air pollution. Even now you can see how that influences our surroundings and but, no character seems to be doing a aspect.

3. Industry

You'd assume that industrial manufacturing would possibly top this list almost about $CO2$ manufacturing but now not pretty. However, it nonetheless produces a massive quantity of it, factoring in at 14%. It want to be mentioned that there are numerous one in each of a type techniques that definitely produce CO2 through easy chemical reactions and do not contain fossil gasoline combustion. This consists of the manufacturing of mineral merchandise which incorporates steel, iron, cement and severa chemical materials.

Whenever we use or do any of those items, we too turn out to be responsible of releasing carbon dioxide into the environment. This is what is called our "carbon footprint" or the sum everyday of the CO2 we produce on a daily foundation and is likewise what we want to significantly reduce.

Now, you is probably thinking, isn't carbon dioxide produced certainly too? What distinction does that make? Yes, it's miles real that CO2 is continuously exchanged among the ocean, the environment and the land itself. It is produced thru a number of living topics which includes animals, flora and various microorganisms. However, without the extra that we produce artificially, the ones natural processes generally typically generally tend to balance itself out, as a result causing no extraordinary trouble by means of any approach.

It grow to be handiest once more in 1750 even as the Industrial Revolution commenced that people have extensively contributed to the upward push of more CO_2 which of path, eventually added about weather alternate.

So why does sustainable power rely? The answer is easy. If we keep dwelling the manner we do, subsequently, the climate changes due to this incessant abuse will bring about drastic environmental and weather modifications - more floods, stronger warmth. It's steady to mention that this will thoroughly spell the death of lifestyles on Earth itself and we have no one else accountable however ourselves.

But it does not want to seem if we start making changes right now. We have masses of various sustainable alternatives and the generation that would permit us harness it is to be had. Shall we check those?

Sustainable Energy Sources

There are many splendid types of sustainable strength, and most of them depend in some manner on sun strength. Hydroelectric similarly to wind electricity are each the give up result of differential heating on the Earth's floor which the ends in the formation of each precipitation and wind due to the truth the air is lifted.

One can also right now make use of sunlight as a manner of powering up their homes. Solar panels had been spherical for pretty a while now and are being utilized in a single-of-a-kind components of the globe. While complete conversion to it is even though inside the midst of being studied, one cannot deny that it's miles the numerous most dependable of renewable energy resources.

Sounds a touch complex, right? Well, to higher apprehend those it's time we took a better observe each alternative.

1. Solar Energy

This form of power deliver uses the nuclear fusion power produced with the aid of way of and within the Sun's middle. Sounds immoderate, does no longer it? This energy can, in fact, be gathered and then implemented in awesome techniques. From using photovoltaic cells (solar panels) to produce power to something more less difficult which includes solar water heating, solar home cooling/warming. While the technology though does now not allow for big-scale use along with powering complete current-day cities, the not unusual domestic can surely benefit from it.

These days, you should buy sun panel kits out of your hardware shop or maybe on-line if you're looking for some thing precise. It does no longer require the know-how of a rocket scientist to position the ones collectively so as long as you understand some fundamental carpentry and facts of a way to use tools, you are right to move. One of those devices can assist lessen your month-to-month electric powered invoice by means of as a minimum 5% or more, relying on what number of and how often it is used.

2. Wind Energy

Now, you may think that harnessing wind strength may want to take a windmill or some component definitely huge this isn't always feasible to have at home. However, this is definitely now not the case. If you live in an area wherein there's a non-prevent go with the flow of wind you then certainly definately should in all likelihood need to strive generating herbal strength via using small-scale mills. These micro-wind or small wind turbines can generate more than enough energy to power your lighting similarly to a number of your commonplace circle of relatives appliances. It all relies upon on how exposed your net internet site is to wind power. There are turbine kits collectively with DIY courses available online so constructing one need to no longer be too hard as well.

Much like sun electricity, it'd also help lessen the amount you pay for strength each month. The percent all relies upon upon the electricity you are able to generate. Some human beings have been able to reduce theirs through the usage of 1/2 of. Aside from this, you furthermore mght get the same government incentives and be paid for the energy you produce even in case you're the one the use of it! Lastly, through the use of a greener supply of power, you'll be capable of reduce your carbon footprint consequently helping in restoring the general fitness of our planet.

three. Hydro (Water) Power

Now, this one you have visible in plenty of various paperwork. Some dams, for one, are able to produce massive quantities of power thru the stress of the water itself. This non-forestall go with the drift of pressurized liquid can be harnessed and transformed into power. For years, people who live near water assets which includes rivers, creeks or even small waterfalls have been the usage of those natural energy property now not just to irrigate but furthermore electricity their farms. Today, this era has been downscaled in order that human beings also can use it to supply strength to their cabins and houses.

From heating and lighting the uses of hydroelectric strength is quite limitless thinking about the supply itself is renewable. If you're leaving off the grid, this is one manner to further lessen the carbon footprint you're making. You may also moreover even make money off of it via the authorities incentives that you will be taking factor in. However, there may be one disadvantage and this is the easy truth that city-dwellers won't be able to enjoy this just however for apparent motives.

While all of these alternatives might in all likelihood have you ever ever dispensing pretty a chunk of cash to get started out out, it's far more essential for us to attention on their long term outcomes. You'll get a return for your funding internal some months of the use of them and after that? It's not some factor but financial financial savings all of the way. Of direction, we can't look beyond the truth that the surroundings would possibly genuinely be thanking you for it as nicely. Remember, stay green and live easy.

Natural Heating and Cooling

Heating and cooling are two of the topics that generally have a tendency to consume up the most power in our domestic as a end result they will be additionally one of the maximum essential culprits that growth our carbon footprints. Luckily, there are greener techniques of undertaking this purpose that could now not most effective assist protect our surroundings-- however offer you with some first-rate economic monetary financial savings as properly.

1. Insulate

Want to preserve your home real warmth within the direction of colder seasons and cool at some point of hotter months? Investing in weatherstripping and insulation is one of the exceptional options to get this accomplished. Sure, getting it installed can value quite a piece of coins but you'll be able to see a go lower back on as a end result in some unspecified time in the future of the 3 hundred and sixty five days in the form of lower energy bills.

2. Natural Shading

Landscaping can play a massive function when it comes to lowering your electricity payments and retaining the temperature in your private home clearly right. You can shop as lots as 40% in cooling in case you use clever landscaping, in your property. Having 3 wooden positioned round your private home in regions wherein the sun receives clearly warmth is powerful in terms of blockading out the warmth. In wintry weather, they permit radiant warmth to skip via therefore maintaining the surroundings exceedingly battle as well.

Shrubs also are awesome additions. They shield the decrease portion of your private home's partitions via blockading out robust sunlight hours. In wintry weather, they act as windbreakers and guard your home from the frigid air. Remember to choose sorts which might be low protection.

three. Blinds and Drapes

Never underestimate the capacity of those to hold your private home warm temperature or cool whenever needed. Two-layered drapes are the maximum inexperienced with regards to cooling at a few degree inside the summers and preserving warm temperature within the route of winters. Blinds, even though now not as effective, moreover gives you more flexibility close to the quantity of moderate you need streaming into your house. If you want a few element greater natural, bamboo blinds is probably actual for this motive as nicely. They are mild-weight, clean to put in and will ultimate you season after season.

Now, permit's communicate approximately how you can get rid of indoors heat for the duration of the summer season. Usually, to do this, human beings may flip their air-conditioning all the manner up or have at the least three fans running at the same time. All of that consumes manner too much power and when you have to do it each unmarried day at some point of hotter seasons? You'll become searching for lots. So what are you capable of do?

1. Roof vents

Ventilating your property's attic can assist in reducing collected warmth which could probable otherwise radiate all over your private home. These vents are pretty a great deal less expensive as properly, beginning from $5 to $10 at most and set up is not even hard to do. They will no longer upload to the loosen up inside the course of an awful lot less warmth months-- but will in truth help in removing moisture from your attic.

2. Ceiling fans

These are inexperienced home coolers but do not use as a whole lot strength as special types of lovers or air conditioners. It charges approximately $1.50 each month to run however can lower the heat in a room considerably. Used along issue your AC, it in reality works even better at frivolously shelling out the cool air. You're searching as a minimum 30% monetary financial financial savings with this.

So there you have had been given it, easy but very effective techniques through which you could keep cash with out the usage of an excessive amount of energy and giving herbal solutions a try.

Green Home Lighting Options

1. CFL: The Better Choice

You've visible those little matters earlier than, they'll be swirly and actually resemble mild serve ice cream. Besides the reality that they're aesthetically specific and are available in an entire lot of numerous shapes, they may be additionally strength inexperienced.

While they charge a bit extra than your commonplace bulb, they final a whole lot longer and are also more steady for they release tons plenty much less warm temperature. These things are so notable, a few cities are giving them to families free of price.

2. LEDS

These will continually be the pinnacle favored for plenty green dwelling parents. They are strength green and really long lasting. They do price a piece more than the CFL's but the blessings are greater too. They use lots much less energy and help lessen your slight energy intake via as an entire lot as 90%. LED's additionally do not embody mercury and lots of cities do recycle those.

3. Daylight

If there can be moderate out and it's miles brilliant sufficient to assist you to carry out your hobby with out straining your eyes then rent it. Keep the blinds and drapes open or in case you're keen on taking subjects a chunk in addition, deploy a skylight in your house.

The quality places would be inside the living room in that you and your circle of relatives can gather inside the path of the day and art work to your coronary coronary heart's content fabric cloth with out flicking any slight on. This easy step will let you keep a large sum of money each yr.

4. Motion sensors and dimmers

For your teenager's rooms, the ones is probably very green. Kids commonly have a tendency to miss to show the lights off each time it isn't in use and that could result in masses of wasted power. However if you have the ones mounted then you definitely wouldn't should fear about that anymore.

You can modify the time the lighting fixtures in reality so each time they may be a few different vicinity within the residence it might definitely dim or turn off by means of itself.

Needless to mention, there are some of awesome technology and upgrades almost about lighting structures that could permit every family to move green. All you want do is look them up and discover which one suits your needs and options the wonderful.

Green Living Tips

Living sustainably and green could no longer absolutely incorporate adding a supply of smooth power to your private home. There are masses of various processes via which you could participate inside the green motion and at the equal time, collect the benefits that typically come from it. To assist you get commenced with some clean subjects that you may do in and round of your own home, beneath is a quick list of a few hints that you may attempt.

1. Transport

As cited in a previous financial disaster, carbon from vehicles has certainly one of the largest influences on our deteriorating environment so you could probably need initially this. There are quite simple but awesome changes that you could do. If you can a few place close by, take your motorbike or simply stroll. You'll be able to exercise and on the identical time, save cash on high-priced gas.

This, on my own, permit you to store masses of bucks each yr. Another element that you could do is arrange a carpool for art work or for taking children to school. It might likely preserve absolutely everyone in your organisation time and money at the identical time as assisting you gather a more potent courting with them. If you can get the complete community to do that, the impact will be even greater.

2. Water

Even in places wherein there's ample rainfall, water despite the truth that becomes an ecological hassle. Clean, potable water is a want and as such, it have to be used efficiently. However, this isn't the case for lots families. What we must all undergo in mind is that every drop of it calls for electricity to clean out and shipping which furthermore equals fossil gasoline emissions.

So what can you do to assist reduce that? Simple subjects along with turning off the tap or shower even as you're now not the usage of it are an great begin. The act by myself might assist you hold gallons of water and in flip, decrease your consumption as properly because of this you may want to pay tons less than the equal antique. For gardening, try and ease up on the usage of the hose and collect rainwater rather. The identical is going for laundry up your vehicles or the the the front porches.

three. Food

You may not assume an lousy lot of it but the food we eat collectively absolutely has a massive effect on our planet. The reasons suit up with that of water, in that power is wanted for it to be produced after which transported worldwide. There are also times wherein the insecticides used for them seep into herbal water, effectively destroying the land itself.

Fortunately, changes are going on on this corporation as properly and people are going all over again to the basics of extra sustainable food systems. The idea behind greener meals can be summed up honestly: "devour community, devour natural, devour seasonal and eat tons less meat." All 4 will guarantee you monetary savings on the subject of your meals budget in addition to better not unusual health now which you're no longer some actual, nutritious meals.

4. Waste Disposal

Some years inside the beyond, waste come to be the maximum crucial environmental trouble that we had to deal with. The solution for it, and to keep away from cluttering the earth with our trash turn out to be to recycle. However, these days, no matter such a number of fantastic troubles cropping up waste stays a big deal. Clutter, loss of place, the strength and assets had to circulate it. It all gives up and this is in which the problem begins offevolved. So separate your waste well, discover ways to recycle and deliver composting a attempt.

All these items, small and clean they might seem, will will let you earn a piece greater cash. Compost sells and there incentives that consist of recycling. The biggest benefit?

You're making higher of use of the waste your household produces.

So there you have got it, sincerely five of the techniques thru which you may be able to reduce your carbon footprint and stay a greener life. There are many unique subjects that you may do, of direction, and it all relies upon upon how big of a trade you are inclined to make. While going actually off the grid is a chunk on the acute aspect for a few, developing extra sustainable sources for your requirements isn't.

Chapter 8: Saving Energy

Every day we waste a whole lot of strength thru the goods we use in our homes. The maximum not unusual example of energy waste is through the usage of incandescent lightbulbs. Though there are extraordinary styles of the ones bulbs, the power that they use to function is normally amongst 60 watts and 100 watts. While you may need the bulb inside the porch to live on, it's going to likely be the use of one hundred watts of power in step with hour and fast growing the payments. Electrical objects together with incandescent bulbs are called Energy Inefficient, because they do not employ to be had energy well, use way more strength than needed, and turn out to be dropping energy and growing your bills. The extraordinary alternative to be had is Energy Efficient devices, which supply the equal (or better!) widespread overall performance on the equal time as saving strength.

For example, fluorescent electricity-saver bulbs offer the equal amount of slight as an incandescent lightbulb at the identical time as using best nine watts to 11 watts of energy in step with hour. To placed this in attitude, incandescent bulb makes use of as masses strength in keeping with hour as six energy inexperienced lightbulbs!

There are 3 sorts of modifications that you will be looking to make so that it will keep money and alternate your power use for the higher:

- Free Changes
- Economic Changes
- Home Energy Retrofit

Free Changes you can make to Save Energy

Free adjustments are modifications that you can make in your cutting-edge way of existence that relate for your current power utilization. These are easy adjustments to make, and will simplest require you to barely regulate your modern-day way of lifestyles to place them into workout. Best of all, you won't must spend any coins to implement those tips and recommendations - you'll be capable of see the modifications for your next energy bill, and could have extra cash in your pocket!

Do no longer leave lighting on whilst they're no longer desired. Lightbulbs may additionally appear to be harmless little electronics, but they could rack up a notably excessive invoice! It's smooth to alternate your conduct in order that whilst you any room in your house you do now not depart the lighting fixtures on. Even in case you recognise that you may be returned in most effective five minutes, it's though well worth taking the time to flip that mild-switch - in the long run, the bulb continues the use of electricity whether or not or no longer you are there or now not!

Do not keep fridge/freezer doors open for too lengthy. Every time which you open a refrigerator or freezer, more power is used. Some human beings have a dependancy of repute with the fridge door open on the equal time as speakme or surfing via it for no purpose. If you need to shop on energy, it doesn't take hundreds to make certain that even as you head for the fridge or freezer earlier of time what you want so you can fast pick out it after which close the door. This is in particular essential in houses with children! Children love setting up the fridge, and frequently leave the door open on the identical time as accomplished - refrigerator locks are an splendid method to this hassle! Another way to increase the overall performance of your fridge is to defrost it frequently (as soon as a month not much less than). While those hints and hints might not look like they might make a good deal difference, a fridge makes use of about 14 percentage of the overall energy a residence uses - so any little reductions in that quantity can also have a severe impact for your energy bill!

Unplug or transfer off virtual home system after you have have been given used them. Many appliances maintain to apply power despite the fact that they may be now not in use. No depend number how little power those home system use on their stand-thru mode, it is nonetheless energy, and you will though need to pay for it. Taking a few greater seconds to plug within the kettle or boiler may be properly really worth it while you get your decreased energy bill on the quit of the month!

Put the pc to sleep! This one is a complex one - despite everything, all of us want to use our computer systems regularly and we're capable of't unplug them all of the time. However, the video show units do use severa energy. Anyone who has a computer is aware about that the battery lasts greater than or 3 instances more whilst the show display is off, because the show takes far extra energy than the CPU. A compromise among ease-of-use and strength payments might be to show the show off each time you aren't the usage of your pc. Luckily, all computer systems have settings that allow them to show the display off routinely at the same time as the pc has not been used for a sure quantity of time - this feature is a protracted manner more energy inexperienced than the use of a screensaver. It will only take a few minutes to alternate the putting to your computer, and you most effective must make this change once!

Turn the thermostat down! Whether you have got were given valuable heating or cooling or a boiler, turning the thermostat down is properly nicely really worth any inconvenience you could experience. After all, it is easy to feature a sweater or take off a layer of clothes as a way to keep your frame snug, and this transformation must have an large effect in your energy bill! As nicely, you do now not need boiling heat water all the time - turn the thermostat all of the way down to your boiler, and if you really want a warm bath then turn it up 10-15 mins earlier than your soak.

Do laundry with bloodless water. The concept of the use of hot water for doing the laundry is tempting, especially within the frigid winters. While that may be right, washing clothes in warm water takes a toll on your payments and pockets. Using cold water as an opportunity will depart your garments absolutely as clean as warm water, and will help you to save sizeable quantities of electricity!

Economic Changes that you could make to Save Energy

Economic changes are number one modifications that you can make to your home, electronics and home gadget with a view to maintain extra and consume a good deal plenty less strength. By making those changes you can see a drastic impact in your strength bills. This segment indicates severa financial adjustments that you can with out problem make in your own home for an exceptionally low preliminary charge.

Firstly, caulk up and draft-evidence your property. Often a large contributor to placing the thermostat is because of the truth most of the cold or warmness air receives in via the openings in the house. These openings ought to include the chimneys, domestic home home windows, and under the doors - all areas that permit your heating or cooling to interrupt out! You can caulk up and seal those starting to ensure that the draft does not get in. As a cease end result, you may not lose hot or cold air so quick, and also you'll have the functionality to turn the electricity of the thermostat down some notches.

Switching to energy saving merchandise is the second one smooth manner to make economic adjustments in your private home. Energy saving electronics use minimal strength and are significantly optimized for average overall performance. While the ones products, like bulbs, can be appear greater expensive initially on the equal time as in evaluation to everyday merchandise, similarly they use loads a lot less power. The prevent result is they make up for their immoderate charge with a enormously extended lifespan and reduces in the electricity invoice.

Lastly, Insulate! Insulation protects your property in competition to the temperature outside thereby similarly decreasing the need to kick back or heat up the house. Insulating your boilers will make sure that the brand new water stays warm for an extended time and that it does now not lose warmth as quick. This trade will further reduce your need to preserve the thermostat up continuously, as insulation will allow the boiler to offer hot water for a long time, even at low temperatures.

The Home Energy Retrofit

Home Energy Retrofitting, additionally referred to as Green Retrofitting, is the technique of making adjustments to your own home an exceptional way to preserve extra strength. Some examples of these adjustments encompass: upgrading to more inexperienced domestic tool, renovating, and insulating. While it can take awhile to discover the coins, upgrading gift electronics and machines that you use to more energy-green ones could have a huge impact to your power bill. The new technology to be had not only reduce strength use, but also permit us to waste a good deal much less water.

Some of those upgrades are easy enough to do-it-yourself at home, at the same time as others can also want professional help. Additional hints for domestic power retrofitting encompass:

- Installing low-float shower heads so that a good buy a good deal much less water is wasted even as you're taking a bathtub

- Using renewable and sustainable strength

- Switching to strength-saving merchandise

- Tuning up your heating and cooling systems and big home equipment

- Making use of inexperienced electricity

- Making use of sun electricity

Going Green

Saving coins is one splendid advantage of going inexperienced, however there are numerous distinct blessings to going inexperienced as properly! The power that we typically use these days (coal, fossil fuels, and so forth.) is non-renewable. These sorts of energy are unfavorable to the surroundings and might only be used a single time - as speedy as they will be lengthy long gone, they'll not come returned. These fuels also are dangerous to the ozone layer and characteristic a massive have an impact on on global warming patterns.

By deciding on to go green for your lifestyles, you could make certain that the arena's fuel belongings will final for an progressed amount of time, that the environment may be blanketed, and that future generations can be able to live in a healthful and inexperienced environment. Renewable power is lots cheaper to harness and produces little to no waste, ensuring restricted environmental damage.

Renewable power merchandise rely upon herbal assets for his or her strength and usually require a completely little protection. Most of those gadgets art work simply as well as non-renewable devices, except that they harvest herbal energy and are often masses lots less expensive to apply.

The predominant types of renewable strength assets are:

- Biomass
- Geothermal Energy
- Hydroelectric Power

Solar Water Heating

While it's far greater power-green to wash your garments in cold water, you can discover it tough to observe this tip if you have a robust desire for washing your clothes with heat water. Others might also moreover moreover have trouble turning off their boiler within the event that they need on the spot access to warm water of their faucets at any time. One manner to encompass the ones picks for your existence whilst being electricity green and saving on bills is to install Solar Water Heating.

In order to make this shift, you'll first need to put in solar water panels. These glass panels are typically set up on the roof, however can be located everywhere out of doors on your private home. Water is pumped as tons because the glass panels in which it's far heated - a mechanism controls the waft simply so the heated water is going down and cold water comes up for heating. This modern manner of heating your water will will let you have regular access to warmness water in your own home without any greater strength fees.

Solar Boilers

The normal boilers we have got at home burn up loads of power because of the reality they constantly heat the water. These boilers are not green in any respect - as speedy as you operate even a small amount of heat water, it is modified proper now within the boiler with cold water. This impacts the overall temperature of the water within the boiler, and requires similarly heating. For instance, in case you take a bath and use half the tank of heated water, the opposite half of is right now whole of bloodless water. This approach modifications the remaining warm water to be simplest mildly warm, which calls for further heating and uses greater strength. If you pick to use a sun boiler as a substitute, this isn't always a problem because it makes use of your solar energy to warmth the water, preventing greater fees.